Women will never make the too' behavior. Change requires thinking and being different. This book will open your eyes to how women themselves create the very situations they want to change and what to do about it. A must read for every woman who wants to reach her full potential. A 21st century manual for women's leadership anywhere in life."

—Nancy O'Keefe
Business Strategist, Executive Coach

As a women's leadership expert, I've been responsible for developing women as Head of the Learning & Development functions for Fortune 500 companies. What I know for sure is this: As we increase the presence of women in business, medicine, politics etc. - we need to know how to be leaders - authentic compassionate leaders. Whether we are leading our own business or a Fortune 500 company, women are uniquely positioned to excel in leadership. Dr. Dorothy brilliantly sets us up for success and gets us to stop playing it safe and instead to play it real. This book will show you how Good Girl syndrome is not going to serve you instead it's the Real Woman that's needed to do the job. Learn how to balance the needs of others vs the needs of self, who you are not and who you are expected to be. Read this book and fall in love with the woman and life you deserve to create.

—Janet Wise, MS HRD
WISE ADVANTAGES

Dorothy takes you on a journey of discovery and awakening. Giving you permission to be true to you and explore what it is that has real meaning and importance to you. She lays out the impact of being the good girl to you (and generations of women that follow.) As you read this book, set aside time to reflect with each chapter. When you do what you uncover will be the gift of being You. Then, go share that person with the world!

—Belinda Pruyne
Leadership Advisor
Business Innovation Group

REAL WOMEN CHANGE THE WORLD:

Letting the Good Girl Die So The Real Woman Can Live

Dorothy A. Martin-Neville, PhD

"Women should take a more active role in society."

"The world will be saved by Western woman."

"If you think you are too small to make a difference,
try sleeping with a mosquito."

Dalai Lama

DEDICATION

This book is dedicated to my sister May who has so beautifully claimed her voice, to my daughter Amy who has very little trouble speaking her mind, and to my nieces Bianca and Katie, and my beautiful niece-in-law Lindsey who is an amazing addition to the family. May they always know the world needs to hear what they have to say.

I also dedicate this book to my two glorious granddaughters, Madison, with her vast love of animals, and Kaitlyn, who is learning how absolutely unlimited she is. May they each continue to learn the value of their voices in changing this world to one where all people demonstrate love and collaboration in walking this world together.

CONTENTS

INTRODUCTION

REAL WOMEN CHANGE THE WORLD: Letting the Good Girl Die So The Real Woman Can Live. Why this title? Several reasons. First, if as the Dalai Lama states, women need to take a more active role in society so that we can be the ones who change the world, we need to quickly grow into the level of influence required to make the changes needed. There is no way we can do that when our voice is not heard or while we hold onto a position of being "nice" or "good" so that we don't "cause trouble" hurt someone's feelings or upset the status quo.

Second, on a personal note, I was raised by a violent father who had no tolerance for anything but what he considered *Good Girl* behavior. Consequently, achieving the goal of becoming the *Good Girl* was considered perfection. To support that, sending me to a Catholic school from 6th-12th grades was considered a great step in reinforcing his teachings. I tried to live up to those standards, even if only for a short while.

Nonetheless, try as I might, having my parents and I required to go to the convent in the evening to meet, yet again, with the principal to discuss my behavior was fairly common. (They were all "innocent" crimes. It was just that I frequently got caught.) In addition, detention became a second home to me. I always got great grades, but I got little credit for that since it was God who gave me the brains. I, however, apparently developed my voice and my ability for passing notes on my own. As I result, I learned early that being alive and real was far more important to me than being good even if there was a frequent price to pay.

Now, I have reached a point in my life where I have lived every item on my extensive bucket list. I consider my intelligence, and spiritual gifts of intuition and inner knowing along with my great faith and sense of humor my most significant qualities. Having traveled far more than most, with friends from all over the world of many races, nationalities, and faiths, I can say I now know what it takes to make our lives ours and our world what it needs to be. The question is whether or not we are willing.

Third, on a professional note, this title is also the result of watching thirty years of women clients, students, and patients come through my doors being caught in the midst of a personal angst of not knowing who they really were, who they could be, or what it would cost them if they ever found out. Sadly, there were those who didn't want to find out since they feared if they became too self-aware they would need to leave their lives and they would lose "everything." Too many women were frightened of "out growing" their husbands so they stopped their own personal growth.

I have seen that sometimes losing everything is required but other times simply changing how you live your life, not where, is all it takes. Regardless, my question to you and them is always "What will it cost you if you never discover the real you, the *Real Woman*? What if you spend your life being the *Good Girl*, afraid of claiming your adulthood, your personal power, and your truth?" You would be like so many women, even those you would least suspect, who are caught between being honest and being nice, (whatever that means!) and therefore stuck in a world where who they truly are doesn't fit.

Let me explain; the *Good Girl* is a byproduct of living everyone else's expectations of who you should be, what you should do, AND how you should do it. You spend your life being defined by a set of societal constraints that are aimed at guaranteeing that you are non-confrontational, not too opinionated, comfortable to be around, not too wordy, and always "pleasant", "good" or "nice."

Under these conditions, your humor is appreciated when it's not threatening or sarcastic; and your opinions are welcomed, but only if they gently agree with the majority. To play it safe, you only turn to other "good" people for advice. Take all sense of malice or abusive parents out of this. Although they do exist, my experience is much more that the *Good Girl* was raised by parents who played it safe, followed the rules as a way of life, and wanted to support their daughter never getting into trouble.

What frequently happens, however, is that by the time that child finishes her education, any desire to experiment, step out of the box, or be outrageous has been squashed so much that she has lost touch with it. Her values and who she should be are well established. Literally, brief moments of rebellion may show up in anger or defiance but they pass quickly.

A *Real Woman* on the other hand, even if raised in the same environment, at some point worked to truly understand what makes her unique, what makes hers tick, to know what she likes, wants, and needs. She knows that there is a price to pay but she is more than willing to pay it. She wants to be seen, heard, and respected, and doesn't accept it when she is ignored, dismissed, or disrespected. She insists on living out of the box and the conditioning that surrounds her. She has the strength to become a pioneer in her field.

Both the *Good Girl* and the *Real Woman* can be very pleasant, funny, and kind. However, the *Real Woman* is also comfortable being that one-of-a-kind trailblazer or a trend-setter. She knows she needs to take risks in order to grow and succeed, and she willingly takes them.

In addition, she usually knows in the core of her being that like-minded, life-long girlfriends are her greatest asset in navigating the many turns in life's journey. Real Women value Real Women knowing none of us can get through this alone. Other women who have your back are a gift beyond words. They tell you like it is and aren't frightened of letting you know when you are messing up or praising you immeasurably when you succeed.

Because the *Real Woman* is frequently the *Good Girl* who has come into her own, as an Executive Leadership Coach, I see the same characteristics of self-betrayal existing whether my clients are very high-powered women in the C Suite (CEO, COO, CFO, etc.) or new entrepreneurs timidly approaching independence. The same forms of inner-conflict appear such as the illusionary victim mindset only the context is different.

Self-betrayal is a problem in our personal lives and our relationships since we have ingrained patterns of behavior regardless of where we are in life, yet it becomes more obvious and detrimental in our work lives when effective leadership is expected from us.

Because of the mixed messages calling us to be powerful and success-ful – yet within constrictive bounds - we can claim that things are "unfair"; we can claim to be the "victim" and assume a "powerless" position, OR we can see the double-bind and learn how to let the *Good Girl* rules and persona die and simply be who we are. Admit it, we have all seen that phony smile we wanted to slap off of someone's face! That phony smile is the mask of self-sabotage and self-betrayal and frequently has tears behind it. It represents everything the *Real Woman* isn't.

That is why this book has been written. It is to help you see, and if needed, make the necessary transformational process of *Good Girl* into *Real Woman*. Similar to the metamorphosis of a caterpillar into a butterfly. The butterfly contains the best of the caterpillar but with so much more power, ability, and freedom.

It is with my greatest permission that all women can go forward, already having many of the answers as well as many of the questions, with the ability to powerfully, intelligently, and mindfully present themselves in any situation as they truly are, a *Real Woman*.

In preparation, especially for the leadership positions within which we will change the world, learning the vast differences between power and control, defiance/conflict vs. healthy confrontation are necessary skills all *Real Women* will be required to develop. And, yes, we must all own our leadership, even if only over our own lives. As we work with and support women from all over the globe of all races, faiths, and nationalities, this one core truth connects us all - we are all a *Real Woman* underneath.

Because this is a spiritual journey, and we are each intrinsically holy and good, we are called to be everything we are capable of being while supporting others in doing the same. Our greatest satisfaction comes from that sense of freedom we have when we have broken through one more barrier, whether physical, intellectual, emotional, or spiritual. For me, that experience is the best ever!

I love that sense of liberation when I have achieved something I was frightened of. It is a big WOW. Satisfaction, self-love, the realization that all those fears and beliefs were not based on reality all flood in at once. I consider dreams your soul's way of calling you to the next step of your journey. Once a dream shows up, it means you are ready. You are ready for the next dream and all the growth that will come in the process of achieving it. For the *Real Woman* there is no limit.

With emotional intelligence, a mindfulness practice, a fully developed set of personal values, and total possession of her purpose, any woman can be a leader. The first step is a sense of self that knows not only that she deserves a seat at the table but also that she knows how to own it and have an impact once she is there.

**Just when the caterpillar thought the world was over,
she became a butterfly.**

CHAPTER ONE

MINDSET

Choose how to see yourself in the world.

Reaching a level of success that you have worked years or even decades to achieve can feel absolutely amazing. Ironically, however, the hardest part can be owning the fact that you belong there; it wasn't luck, you earned it. This is where recognizing the power of your mindset comes in.

Recognizing the beliefs, the expectations, and the inner messages, you learned long ago, that can greatly impact your ability for success and enjoying the achievements you deserve, is imperative. I have worked with women who were absolutely amazing and yet nonetheless feared being "discovered" as frauds.

That is a set-up for failure before you start. Walking in fear and uncertainty prevents your creative juices from flowing freely. Creativity, intuition, and a sixth sense are your greatest and deepest skills – so you need immediate access.

It can be hard to realize that your long CV, your outstanding resume, and your great ability to work an interview are only small parts of why you got the position you did. You got it because of who you are. Your energy, your way of looking at things, your ability to stand out and be exceptional, are really what got you hired.

1

If you are an entrepreneur, these are the traits that will make your company a wild success. There are hundreds, if not thousands, of others offering the services you offer. What makes you special? YOU. The way you think; the way you choose to brand yourself, the way you choose to make yourself seen, are what sell you.

Simply put, what makes you the success you are, are the qualities you possess in the way only you possess them. Those are your definitive factors.

Let's start by looking at the *Good Girl* because she may be the greatest saboteur you've got. No matter how much you develop, she is still within you. The power you give her is the deciding factor on her impact. It lets you know how far you have come as well as how far you still need to go.

The *Good Girl* is someone who was raised to make sure she never made anyone feel uncomfortable. She was raised to never offer an unpopular or contrary opinion on any topic because she would risk offending someone. Always, she put others' feelings, wants and desires first because that's what a *Good Girl* does. Most importantly she wants and needs everyone to like her. That is her validation that she has done everything right and is therefore lovable. As a child, when she did something wrong she was sent to her room and usually felt unlovable and unwanted. She learned how to behave in order to feel loved all the time. Outrageous, out-of-the-box, uninhibited, "bossy" behavior was never appropriate.

She couldn't stand out or draw attention to herself since that was egotistical. Fitting in was the goal. Think of that picture that floats through Facebook again and again of a little girl in ballet class who is the only one upside down. Notice how many respond and say, "I want to be her." There's a reason. We all want to be that girl who has the strength to simply be – not against- not for – just be - natural and alive.

As she develops, the *Good Girl* usually reaches a point where she realizes she has no idea who she is, what she thinks, what she feels, or what she wants. She realizes her life has been spent focusing solely outside, on others. She has disappeared from her own consciousness.

Discovering, or rediscovering, who she is, what she wants, and what her dreams are become the necessities for reclaiming or creating a life with room for her in it.

This process becomes her metamorphosis and can be absolutely terrifying yet compelling.

The *Real Woman* is frequently the Good Girl who has come into her own. Therefore, she is equally compassionate, kind, and thoughtful. She however is fully present to herself as well as to others. She knows who she is and much of the time she knows exactly what she wants.

It's because she may have struggled to exist that she is aware of what she wants to achieve, who she wants to be, and what her dreams are. She is writing her bucket list and intends to live it. There is a cleanness to her thinking since she doesn't have to distort her ideas to fit others' expectations of who she should be.

When the *Real Woman* speaks, she speaks her truth. It may be filtered for her audience in terms of technical terminology, or to meet them where they are, but she is not filtering herself. This is who she is, what she thinks etc.

I frequently say, "Don't ask me a question, if you don't want an answer." I do so because more than once someone has asked me my opinion and then been offended when it wasn't the same as theirs. If you ask me for my thoughts, my assumption will be that you want to know my truth. If you are simply looking for validation, please tell me. I may validate your opinion, but I may also simply say "That is another approach." No judgment, just a fact – but real.

If I don't offer an opinion it is because it is irrelevant or because I don't want to get into a long-drawn-out debate. I am very comfortable with letting others have their opinions knowing I disagree and that is OK. Are you?

When you are real and comfortable with your own thoughts, you don't need validation through the approval of others. You may share your thoughts, so you can expand your ideas in the sharing or possibly because it can cause you to consider other opinions, but never because you doubt them or have a need to defend them.

Please know I am making a clear distinction here between an honest, undefended *Real Woman* who has nothing to prove; who is comfortable in her own skin, and who has done a significant amount of work on herself to become the woman she wants to be. That is dramatically different from the woman who says she is "real" when in truth she is highly defensive, angry, and in fear of being controlled or manipulated.

This last woman often calls herself "real" yet actually sees no difference between attack and confrontation, between compromise and surrender, or between control and power. Her fear projects her anger, her lack of self-awareness, and her inability to stand comfortably in her own skin without a readiness to battle anyone and everyone who she believes is challenging her. She is hell bent on fighting against the role of *Good Girl* rather than simply standing solidly in the powerful place of the *Real Woman*. As long as she is in an inner battle, she can't be at peace in her own truth.

The *Real Woman* has nothing to defend against. She has no need to be battle-ready. She has peace, power, clarity, and purpose. When she needs to stand up for herself she does so but without a single inclination to do battle or take control. Sometimes that requires a moment to step back and breathe but with experience she knows that and so she does. Simple, but not always easy.

Truthfully, powerful people have no need, or desire, to control. Only people in fear seek to control. Think about it. When an acknowledged national president knows he or she is the leader, they simply discuss/ present their ideas and offer a policy to be followed with the support of their citizens. On the contrary, when a dictator fears a coup, he calls for martial law, controlling everyone's movement in order to safeguard his own position. He cannot lead his people; they will not willingly follow, so he needs to control them through intimidation and fear.

I recognize that fear is a part of all our lives. Fear of a new responsibility. Fear of a medical diagnosis. Fear of being late. Fear of a major presentation that's coming up... As a result, it's highly beneficial to acknowledge fear and learn how to use it or minimize it versus running from it, or letting it run you. We all have fear, yet you can decide how much power you give it in your life. That is totally your choice. Learn how you can best govern it since you have so much else that needs to get done.

Right now, we need far more women in medicine, business, and politics. However, we need those women to balance out the power that already exists in those areas so that we can have the best of both worlds, male and female. We want and need more women Presidents/CEOs of hospitals, insurance companies, and medical clinics. They can bring the heart and soul back to medicine since it needs to be a caring as well as a profitable business.

We also want more women Presidents/CEOs not just in Fortune 100 and Fortune 500 companies but in all the other companies, NGOs, and nonprofits of this world. A woman's tendency is to collaborate, to work for solutions, rather than to win. This can bring humanity back into organizations that are placing radically inhumane demands on their employees. Long hours with no balance of time for family, and/or personal health, are only some of the issues we need to assess.

To support that change, the employees must be considered the first customers of any organization. Conscious capitalism and socially conscious and purpose-driven companies have listened and are all proponents of what is being demanded now by both millennials and the increasing number of women in leadership. This demanded balance comes from a new set of values where heart and head work together. Life is shifting as it always does so why not be a driver of that shift to assure your values are a part of it?

In the political world, we certainly need more women. Someday there will be a woman president but, in the meantime, we need more women in Congress. We need more women in state and local politics as well.

One authority on the subject of women in politics is Barbara Boxer, author of **Nine and Counting: The Women of the Senate.** From her book summary on Amazon:

> The Women of the United States Senate have forever changed the political landscape. Their backgrounds, personal styles, and political ideals may be as diverse as the nation they serve. Yet they share a commonality that runs deeper than politics or geography -- they desire to give a voice to all their constituents while serving as role models for women young and old. https://www.amazon. com/Nine-Counting-Senate-Barbara-Boxer/dp/0060957069

It was these women of the Senate who are credited with ending the government shut-down in 2013. After weeks of not being able to accomplish anything while each party aggressively stuck to their own side of the aisle, the women of both parties got together, devised a plan where everyone won a little, and within days the crisis was over. To this day, these women meet monthly for dinner to discuss issues, family, life, and politics. Collaboration, not winning, is their goal. They do it together, as one group of invested women, not party members. This needs to be the politics of the future and as this example shows, this approach is generally women led.

Not for a single moment do I think all women are qualified for the positions they occupy, nor that all women work from the healthiest of motivations or intents. However, I do know that the vast majority of women use power differently than men – not better – differently. We need the mix of approaches for the greater good.

I also know that simply having a woman in a high level position, whether in medicine, business, or politics, doesn't guarantee positive results unless she is a powerful woman, a *Real Woman*, willing and ready to make an impact, to stand out, and to make a difference.

That's because positioning is only the first step. I once worked with a woman who was highly successful on Wall Street. She was CEO of her own firm. When she became, through a series of unexpected turns, the CEO of the American division of a global operation, it was her task to merge several companies into one.

We could easily work together to create a new culture, to decide who fit and who didn't fit that culture, what to outsource and what departments to keep in house. Of all the problems she needed to face, however, the most unnerving for her was that the SVPs of the other organizations didn't like her. They resented her success and that their boss was let go. That is a *Good Girl* problem and it was sabotaging her success.

Another woman who had made it to the C Suite was caught in a dilemma when a colleague presented her idea as his own at a meeting. Should she angrily and righteously confront him and claim the idea as her own, or disappear and slide down her seat? Either way would result in her readily being dismissed.

Thankfully, she was inspired to sit up straight and say in a normal conversational and yet powerful tone with certainty in her voice," Bill, you presented my proposal nicely, but you forgot the key point that brings it all together. I want to add…." There was no key point here really, other than the impression she made to the group.

All in that room could see, without pointing a single finger, whose proposal it was. No acting out, no degrading herself, simply claiming her place at the table and making quite an impact while doing it. Her mindset was defined – "I am not a victim here, I am not powerless, even when fair has nothing to do with it. "

Life isn't fair, yet you need to have the mindset that sets it up to be fair wherever and whenever you can. If Bill was offended, humiliated, or hurt, that was not her intent. Keeping her mouth shut, however, to be a *Good Girl*, would have been a huge act of self-betrayal. She claimed her place, and she will need to again and again - until she doesn't…

Self-betrayal, whether in order to be liked, or to be kind, is a self-inflicted cruelty. People cannot respect you if they don't even know who you truly are. Hiding behind outdated protocols prevents you from being seen. Every one of these points below sets you up to fail or puts you in a situation where you will be betraying yourself without realizing it. In addition, each sabotages your desire to be seen as credible, powerful, and *real*. Which is your weakness?

BEING "NICE":

- Keeps you silent when you have something of value to offer
- Allows others to be valued when it is your opinion they are promoting
- Keeps you in a "one-down" position
- Has you striving to be liked rather than respected
- Keeps you in a child state rather than owning your space and your voice.

"PROVING" YOUR WORTH:

- Doesn't work - It sets you up as one-down before you start
- Is futile - those who don't want to see won't – those who are open, already do
- Doesn't allow your success to speak for itself
- Shows you don't believe you simply belong
- Hides the needed confidence, focus, clear-sightedness, and acknowledgement that you earned your place at the table.

"PLAYING THE PART:"

- There is no "part"
- This takes place when you misconstrue who you already are
- Is supported by aggression, will, ego, and unrealistic expectations
- Prevents authenticity

- Doesn't allow you to bring all of yourself to the table.

The confidence that comes when you have permission, from you, to be your whole, authentic self, while you continue to evolve and grow, sets you free to reach beyond your imagination. As an example, research shows that when men apply for a position they believe having 60% of the job skills required is sufficient since they believe they will learn any other skills they need while on the job. Women, however, believe they need to have 100% of the skills listed already developed.

Not only does this hold you back from moving forward, it also sets you up to never be considered. Don't be nice, shy, or hesitant; be motivated! Every move up the ladder will ask more of you both in terms of skills and leadership ability. That is how you grow. You are becoming more of who you are capable of being, more and more your real self, while gaining more experience. Take a risk - go for it!

Risk is a major part of the growth needed. When I am confronted with something I feel called to and can see my shadow side trying to talk me out of it, I always ask myself the questions: What is the worst thing that could happen? What is the best thing that could happen? No matter what occurs, I have usually already been there through this step, so I am more prepared than not.

Understand, a willingness to take risks:

- Opens up more opportunities
- Provides far more growth
- Frees you from your comfort zone
- Allows you to live not survive.

You learned early in life to live up or down to others' expectations. A higher position brings in higher expectations for you so you need to keep reaching; you need to keep growing into those expectations. Joy, self-confidence, and greater skills will come in proportion to your willingness to jump in, to grow, and to expand your vision.

Be sure to love who you are at the moment and be grateful for what you have done but always know that your past was only your preparation for your future. What's next? What's your vision? What's going to make you the best you that you can be?

Too many have abandoned their passion, their joy, and their outrageous wild side.

No wonder so many women feel incomplete. Parts of themselves were lost because their focus was external - not about living their best self, their highest values, and their visions for themselves or their purpose in this life.

Your best expression of the *Real Woman* is a byproduct of living your truth, taking those risks, owning your power, creativity, and unique skills in service to others. It requires that all of who you are to be present, even those parts you may have left behind.

I am not at all saying anywhere in this book that all, or any, woman should be career-focused, family-focused, or anything else. What I am saying is that no matter what you choose to do with your life, be the leader in that decision. At that point you will always know, without exception, that wherever you are is where you have chosen to be.

Even if you don't like a particular place, either you leave, or you are choosing to stay, so there is no victim. At that point you will need to find what makes it far more than bearable and go after that extra piece.

Perhaps you are tending to a sick parent. If you don't like it, stop. If you don't stop, it's a choice. More than once that statement has initially angered someone. It takes away the grandiosity of martyrdom. I feel no guilt about making the statement however because it's a fact. Being kind is wonderful, but measuring the amount of misery it is costing you doesn't make you a saint, only a complainer, even if it's all internal.

In that instance, can you give yourself permission to go out to play with friends one or two nights a week? Can you take daily yoga classes nearby while you have a helper come in? Be the leader of your choices and their consequences. Anything else is self-betrayal, giving you permission to play a role of doing "good", while being a "victim", and playing "poor me." Anyone practicing introspection won't buy it.

It is such a vast difference from, "I couldn't live with any other decision, so I am going to make the best of it and still bring in laughter, play, and personal time to live my life while I do what I want to do as well as what I feel obligated to do."

Your mindset defines everything. It is absolutely amazing how changing your perspective can completely change your life - professionally and/or personally.

GETTING REAL:

1. Do you know the beliefs that can sabotage you as a *Real Woman*?

2. Have you developed a means of counterbalancing them when they show up?

3. What risks have you taken over your lifetime to succeed or achieve a goal?

4. What happened when you did?

5. What was the cost?

CHAPTER TWO

COMMUNICATION SKILLS

Letting them hear the Real Woman's voice.

After mindset, communication style is where the largest amount of self-sabotage takes place for women. It is where you can at times literally hear the differences between the *Good Girl* and the *Real Woman*. A huge awareness I have that struck me years ago, in regard to voice, is that I have seen many women struggle to speak with confidence. I want to say this clearly – no matter what the "experts" say - do not struggle for CONFIDENCE – it is the middle of the road. My desire for you is to reach far higher. Always speak with CERTAINTY.

Certainty is the cellular knowing that you know what you are talking about. You know who you are. You know what you want to accomplish, even if you are looking for information because you are trying to discover the best options for something. Do not be tentative, frightened, confused, or child-like in your speech. Know in your certainty that you would like additional information, so you can make an intelligent decision. Then simply ask. You deserve that level of credibility and comfort in asking. Notice how frequently women become young children when asking a question. Adult women can ask questions also!

In a sharp contrast to this approach, I have spoken to women whose tone was literally that of a three or four-year-old. Chances are high you have as well. These women want to be taken seriously and seen as *Real Women,* yet it can be difficult for others to do so because they are sending a mixed message. They are saying "I want to sound like a sweet little *Good Girl,* so you will like me, but I also want you to know I am an intelligent, mature, woman." Imagine all those who have written her off immediately. I know I have in the past since that was not the representation I wanted for me or any of my companies.

As a psychotherapist and energy healer, my first thought in assessing this is of a trauma that has them stuck verbally at a certain age of development in which they had no voice. However, there is no room for mixed messages as we grow. We need to do our inner work so that our outer presentation shows who we want to be and how we want to be seen. What we know is that *Good Girls* often maintain the status quo while *Real Women* are changing the world and people believe what they see and hear, not necessarily what we say.

You need to do all you can to achieve the *Real Woman* level of development. Another challenge that comes with the mixed message of the *Good Girl* is that when you are a *Real Woman* you need to accept that not everyone will like you. You are the threat that says another way is possible. For such a young sounding *Good Girl* the idea of intentionally not being liked would feel as if she had done something wrong. If we are emotionally healthy and real, it is never our desire to hurt, offend, or be unlikable, only an accepted reality that it does happen.

I have also heard others whose tone was of a 12 or 13-year-old. After hearing them on the phone and then meeting them I was shocked. I anticipated perhaps an 18-year-old who was still growing versus a woman in her 30's, 40's, or 50's who was trying to appear professional. This adolescent-like voice is still part of the *Good Girl* syndrome and she needs support in claiming her voice and her power.

There are voice lessons that can support women in changing their tone. They are used frequently by those doing commercials, public speaking, audio books, and leadership development. We all have detrimental elements to work with. If this is one of yours, I encourage you to claim your power in your voice as soon as possible. Obviously, I am not speaking about those who have had surgery etc. then your voice is part of your story, and your power-filled energy will need to define you.

In addition to tone, powerful and/or weak energies are experienced through your voice. To be heard as a powerful, authentic, *Real Woman*, requires you to comfortably own that power, and resonate it, verbally, with certainty. For most of us, that authenticity and power develops one risk, one outrageous step after another.

A powerful voice (not loud - but power-filled.) demonstrates that we have learned a great deal about ourselves, our values, and what we want to do, as well as how we do it. In addition, it implies, we have also learned who we don't want to be, what values are not ours, and how we don't want to present ourselves. There is a confidence and self-awareness in the presentation.

Sadly, the self-image of many women is negative or unsure (regardless of what they proclaim.) I find that many women can go to one of two extremes, either spending their language apologizing as a way of life or attempting to blow-over any opposition they encounter, perceived or otherwise. Next time you attend a conference, a networking event, or a meeting spend time observing and listening to others. You will see or hear what I mean. It's intriguing.

It is amazing what you can learn simply by listening. Listen to yourself as well. None of us are done growing until we go Home so we can all slip into one of these habits listed below without realizing it. Just notice and then, without judgement or self-hatred, begin to change where it's needed.

Notice:

Apologizing:

- 'I'm sorry but I missed that, could you please repeat what you said?"

- "I'm sorry but is that seat available?"

- "I'm sorry what time is the meeting?"

- "I'm sorry but I can't."

- What are you actually saying is, "I'm sorry I take up space."

Patterns have power, consciously and unconsciously, and they solidify how we see ourselves in the world. To some this may seem like semantics. However, when we as women are learning how to stand tall in a world that is frequently about power-over we need to own our power verbally, energetically, and consciously, without buying into the power-over illusion.

Sit quietly and notice as you speak each of these phrases below, the powerful difference in tone and energy that occurs simply in changing each of the above to saying:

- "I missed what you said, could you please repeat that?"

- "Is that seat next to you available?"

- "Would you happen to know the time of the meeting?"

- "'I'm not going to be able to ...."

- "What you are actually saying is 'Hello, I would like to actively participate."

Think of how each experience above feels. Try saying each of the variations twice. You can say each of the bottom phrases with kindness or compassion in your voice while still maintaining a powerful presentation.

I absolutely believe in being polite and having honest humility. However, I do not at all believe in making ourselves small. This is significant because speaking from your heart and your power combined rather than apologizing changes how you hold yourself and how others see you.

Men will look at you differently if you are frequently apologizing. They will view you as weak, not an equal. That is not the impression you want to leave. You need to live consciously and mindfully, aware of how your speech patterns impact you as well as others.

Women, because they are conditioned to seeing the world through a different lens, rarely notice the impact their communication style has on others, especially in business. In the words of one theorist, we are gatherers. We want to bring everyone into the fold, so we welcome them with every explanation possible about everything imaginable. All of that so they will feel welcomed and included when a simple word of welcome would suffice, and is frequently all that is wanted.

Learn the points below:

In language:

- Over-explaining is another sign of weakness. Be concise, clear, focused, and on-target

- When you can say it in 12 words instead of 40, do so

- Avoid all weak, tentative words such as "maybe", "possibly", "sort of", "I think"

- Leave out the back-story unless it's asked for – and it rarely is

- Know you belong – don't justify your presence

- Expect to be heard – don't hope to be heard – speak with power/certainty

- Learn to listen – to what is said and what is not said

- You can never take back something you said in haste- so don't

- Respond – never react – watch the movie, don't be in it.

Along these lines, watch the difference between power and aggression. Aggression is ***always*** a defensive mode. To say, 'That is just my style." doesn't change the fact; aggression is always a defensive move.

Now is a really good time to change your style. Either you are trying to prove a point, usually about your worth, your perspective, or your rights, or you are protecting yourself from a perceived enemy.

Let go of the image of enemy. You will have competition, opposing views, even detractors but not enemies. They are rare and in most instances a byproduct of your mindset. Defensive plays in business and in life rarely prove your power, only your fear.

Notice that *Real Women* are seen as powerful, clean, clear, and concise in their communication. Kind and generous usually go in there as well. I believe in every cell of my body that all people are embodied souls, intrinsically holy and good. Some believe that about themselves while others don't. Do you? Do you see your intrinsic goodness?

As we increase the presence of women in medicine, business, and politics, we all need to know how to be leaders in these fields. You need to know how not to let that absolutely intimidating coworker shut you up. You need to not allow fear of the group disagreeing with you cause you to stay silent. You need to let go of the fear of appearing "too smart" or "too invested" and just speak.

You need to learn to pursue any position you want because you deserve to be considered if you want it. It doesn't matter if someone else has more time, experience etc., you may have the one definitive trait they are looking for and which they value more highly than the obvious skills.

Even if a potential woman applicant was far more qualified than the man who got the job, if she never applied, she set herself up to fail. Having permission to go after what you want, to speak up for yourself - is a strong communication style. It is also one many women need to master. No one knows your wants unless you tell them. No one knows you're serious about wanting a change unless you ask for it.

Yesterday, in speaking to a client who has a very successful business, who travels the country speaking, who has teams of men working for her, I was able to see another side to her personality few would believe exists. With 2 grown children and a husband, she has spent her marriage asking for someone to help put the garbage out, set the table, etc. etc. etc. with no response.

At the moment she has a leg that is broken in several places and as a result is confined to the couch. This powerhouse is going crazy stuck in one place. To make the story short, she asked her twenty-something daughter to take the garbage out since the house was starting to smell. The daughter, as could be expected, said she didn't smell anything and kept walking. My client, humiliated in saying so, said she "lost it."

She screamed, yelled, hollered, and sobbed leaving her daughter absolutely baffled since this is a whole new reaction. Sarcasm is my client's normal, and only, response not screeching or even crying. Two hours later her daughter came in the room and apologized asking what else she could do. As you can imagine, word spread, and her husband and son did the same. Her question to me was if she was expected to react that way from now on.

It's a possibility but that will lose force as time goes on. A much better approach is: "Please take the garbage out now since it is starting to smell." Said with power and expectation. "Later." doesn't work, "now thanks" with expectation not hope. I find it amazing that using power, and expectation, in our voice can create miracles.

Not anger, or threats, hope or pleading, but **power and expectation**. Sometimes you simply need to retrain those in your life that you exist since it is you who taught them otherwise in the first place. Training isn't always easy, but it is always necessary.

When my children were teenagers, one evening after a long day at work and after filling a dozen different needs of theirs with no assistance, I refused to cook dinner since, as I told them, "I am tired of doing one-way relationships." After they questioned my sanity, they saw my point. I didn't say they liked it, but they saw my point. Problem solved…... Setting the table and peeling potatoes was never so easy as we talked and laughed at my willingness to make a point. Most women will not. They cannot justify it. As if it needed to be justified.

Women usually resist making such a point because frequently there is a price for communicating your needs and wants. I assure you, there is a far greater price when you don't. Resentment, anger, loneliness, and a loss of the possibility for real relationships that feed everyone develop. No one wins when there is only room for one in the relationship. Risk and communication are the needed keys to change things.

An important point to see here is that, contrary to what some want to believe, you do not behave differently in different locations such as home vs. office. You can try wearing a mask for a few hours at the office but it soon collapses and the "normal" you shows up or at the least I should say, the woman you have chosen to be at this point in your life shows up.

With the corrected mindset of wanting to be the best you, you can be, it requires the ability to communicate powerfully, clearly, concisely, with your heart, head, and soul radiating. It is then that you are the most *Real Woman* imaginable.

You are never done growing, changing, and, becoming more, better, and whole. The best you can do is your best at any moment. It does mean letting that *Good Girl* persona, and everyone else's expectations of who you should be die. Create your own expectations for you and go after them. Others will follow. The *Good Girl* will hold you back, internally and in the world, the *Real Woman,* however, will give you credibility while creating opportunities beyond your imagination.

My first book ***Dreams are Only the Beginning: Becoming Who You are Meant to Be***, speaks of the hundreds of dreams you may have in any one lifetime. It speaks of each of those dreams as being your soul's way of calling you forward, calling you to become everything you are meant to be. When you think of it, how could anyone else know those dreams? They are between you, your soul, and Spirit.

Follow those dreams, you have no idea the you, you will discover along the way. It is an unbelievable way to live your life. It is about discovering the real, authentic you, and coming alive in ways you never imagined possible.

GETTING REAL:

1. How do you communicate with you?

2. Is it mostly judgmental?

3. If so, how can you counter that message?

4. How do you communicate with others?

   Demanding? Controlling? (However, you justify it.)

   Apologetically? Timidly?

5. How do you communicate to the world that you are a leader?

CHAPTER THREE

MINDFULNESS

Becoming aware of your own experience in the moment.

With the absolutely packed lifestyle we have developed in the west, partly because of immediate access to media and the internet, it is too easy for you to get lost in your day. You need to give yourself permission to stop, to disengage, and to find peace within while separating from the noise. Mindfulness is a glorious way to do just that. For me, it is a way of life although I do stop at least twice a day to simply experience being in that space. I find it refines my mindset and locks it in a healthy place. It also allows me to hear all of the conversations going on, inner and outer.

In the morning, before getting out of bed, I practice mindfulness by going into the silence within and assessing how I am feeling. How do I feel emotionally and physically? Did I wake up stressed? Depressed? Excited? Tired? Refreshed? It allows me to focus and intentionally come fully alive to face my day.

In the evening, I review my day, not the pragmatic details but my experiences, did I betray myself, was I in joy? Fear? (If so why? What story had I told myself?)

The need for such a practice has existed for millenniums. I see mindfulness as the latest form of meditation or reflection. It calls you to quiet all else and listen solely to your inner-world. Amazingly, and perhaps ironically, it is also the best way to experience the outer-world. When you can block out all the stimuli around you, and experience the world within, you come to see yourself as in this world but not of it. You are far bigger than the world you have created for yourself which is why you cannot let it define you. Just keep growing beyond it...

Through mindfulness you disconnect from the world. You find peace in the quietness of your own soul or essence. You remember your purpose, observe your growth, and recognize beliefs that may be holding you back from becoming more of who you are called to be.

The initial obvious gifts of practicing mindfulness are the peace and relaxation. The gifts increase over time to provide a much greater sense of the you that exists apart from all else. For those who have lost themselves in the demands of others, it is a wonderful way to rediscover the you that still exists.

By momentarily disassociating and stepping out of the drama and often self-created stresses, (**the story**)**,** you are able to see your part in them, whether you began the drama or are perpetuating it. You are then able to let go of blame, victim, and imaginary "stuckness" so that you can see options and other perspectives. You can end the drama in your life immediately. Or, if it is drama created by others you can step out of it and simply choose not to play. The answers for how to do it all appear in the silence.

One obvious clue to identify those who have mastered this practice is completely noticeable in a crisis. When life around them is truly traumatic, they go within, detaching from the rush and panic. They are not ignoring it; they are simply not getting caught up in the energetic chaos that is immobilizing others. They resonate strength, balance, and a clear perspective on how to handle the situation. They don't react; they respond. They quickly assess the situation, and then question what assets are available, what needs to be done, and decide what the most effective and efficient way to handle it is. The reality is, this could be any one of us. You can simply, even if not easily, choose to stand straight, find that inner strength and be that powerful, reality-based, mindful, woman you are called to be in any situation.

Unfortunately, the other option is self-betrayal, playing the victim, being emotionally overwhelmed, letting fear overtake you, going into powerlessness, and believing you are not able to deal with the world around you. You become the fragile woman who needs to be rescued. I find that image soooo offensive yet unfortunately so common. No woman in her truth fits that description. No woman is incapable of handling her life unless she chooses to be.

The *Good Girl* frequently spends too many years disconnecting from her own innate strength, wisdom, and creativity in order to be the supportive agent of the "other." She loses touch with all of her own capabilities including her capability to support herself. She may move mountains for others but believes she has no strength or ability to help herself or, perhaps more honestly, no justification.

As an energy practitioner, I used to tell my clients to go within while I worked on them, balancing their energy fields and removing any blockages or diseases I found. Pretty consistently, they would cry telling me that in the silence they remembered so many things. They felt so many things that they just realized they had forgotten who they really were in the chaos and the demands that had become their life.

On a larger scale, a universal practice of Mindfulness could be a major cultural change agent calling every one of us to live a balanced, centered, and peace-filled life. What a different world that would be.... Could you imagine if every woman on this planet were to realize her completely unlimited capabilities?

It truly doesn't matter if your call as a *Real Woman* is to homeschool your children, become president of your country, start a multi-billion-dollar company or open a local farmers-market and planting-station for all those in your town who need or want to grow their own food. No job is any more important or significant than another. All are needed. The difference is in how you are doing it. Where are you coming from when you do it?

Mindfulness is how you know. Not in your head or in your logic but in your experience of living in your truth. That only comes from being fully present in your body. You KNOW it on a cellular level. Are you doing what you "should" do or what you are called to do? Are you in resentment or joy?

I pray you have had at least one experience when you felt, yes felt, that something was right, or conversely, that something was wrong. The problem is that for so many of us more times than not we ignore that inner knowing, that inner bell saying Stop, Look, Don't Listen, Move Away NOW!

It doesn't matter if it's around a piece of cake, a new man in your life, a job offer that feels "off" or anything else. If you haven't already, you must learn to listen to and trust yourself far more than trusting anyone else. I love people. I truly do. It's why I have done the work I have done for decades. I especially love watching them grow, watching them "get it" and I know the difference this awareness makes.

Know you also deserve to live life loving what you are doing and loving who you are while doing it. Take this tool, this Mindfulness practice, and make it an integral part of your gift to yourself. Start with 10 minutes each morning and each evening. OK - do 5 minutes if that seems horrifically long. Use that time to catch up with you. Expand the time as you desire.

As I said, for me the morning session is the preparatory stage for my day. It brings balance, quiet and calm as I walk into the day.

In the evening, Mindfulness becomes a time of reflection. Did I feel frightened, excited, uncomfortable in my own skin? It shows me who I was that day. Did someone offer me an opportunity that will cause me to grow? Did I take it?

In response to the day's events, did I fall into the false humility of the *Good Girl* at any point and feel yucky in my body or did I live my truth as a powerful and *Real Woman*? Try it on yourself....

With practice, you truly show up in your life and you know you are at home so that your evolution takes place naturally.

To summarize, Mindfulness supports:

- Acceptance
- Respect
- Trust
- Connection
- Intimacy with self and others
- Safety
- Humor
- Play
- The ability to laugh at yourself
- Following your dreams and your purpose
- You, in recognizing the differences in how the *Good Girl* vs a *Real Woman* feels.

This life is meant to be lived, not survived. If you are going to go through it, living as wildly and outrageously as you are called to, then you need to be the director of the journey as well as the passenger.

Others cannot tell you where you belong or who you should be. Only you can discover that as you go along. Only you can discover your dreams and your inner callings. Remember that!

There will be fear, there will be logical reasons to stop for a moment and reassess what you are doing and why. So do it - stop - briefly. Never, however, will there be moments to surrender your passion, your vibrancy, or your love of life.

Collapse in drama if you need, or want to, for a few minutes on occasion or even for a few hours with girlfriends and a bottle or two or three of wine (depending upon the number of girlfriends.). The drama, the tears, the misery, the self-pity, and the wailing and gnashing of teeth, can be cathartic. Then, as Cher said, "Snap out of it!"

GETTING REAL:

1. How did you wake up this morning?

   Sad? Joyful? Tired? Refreshed?

2. Are you frightened of the silence?

3. How could mindfulness support you and your lifestyle?

   Eliminate drama? Create peace?

4. Have you used it yet to fall in love with the silence within?

5. Can you see yourself as separate from the world around you?

CHAPTER FOUR

EMOTIONAL INTELLIGENCE

Understanding your emotions without being led by them.

One of the real differentiators between the *Good Girl* and the *Real Woman* that I have seen is in their focus for developing Emotional Intelligence (EI.) Let me start by saying that this term refers to your knowing, intelligence, and understanding of emotions. Great questions to ask yourself to assess your EI are: What triggers you? What wounds you? Do you "run"? Do you collapse when challenged? Do you know the answers to these?

I have found that the *Good Girl* has focused her development of EI on understanding the "other" whoever that may be. Because she wants to be considered good and thus worthy of love she believes this level of understanding is what will make her lovable, and thus "good enough." As a result, she focuses solely and intensely on what others want and/or need.

The *Real Woman* may have a similar understanding of others, or close to it, but her primary area of development is focused on her EI about herself. Her understanding is that self-awareness is key to the career and relationships she wants.

A crucial point to differentiate in relationship to EI is that possessing not just self-awareness but also self-honesty is the additional imperative. You have to be honest with yourself if you are to have healthy emotional intelligence in your relationships. Denying traits or patterns you don't like about yourself always comes back to bite you. Own them and only then can you deal with them. A developed sense of self-awareness, self-acceptance, and understanding of your own emotional triggers and strengths provides a wealth of information that prevents blame, judgment, and accusations of others and makes exceptional and well-deserved relationships possible.

I am not saying that either one has a monopoly on EI. Again, you are never done until you go Home. It is more that each style has developed a different area of expertise within Emotional Intelligence.

The *Good Girl* may understand others very well because her focus has been so outward toward making others feel comfortable, happy, content, etc. but she has spent very little time learning about her own emotional life and needs as a result. She may actually have avoided them. Consequently, she has immense EI but only in reading others.

She can, and does, anticipate others' needs and fill them before they ask. She struggles to never forget another's needs or wants and feels guilty when she does even if it is because she is so overwhelmed from servitude that things fall through the cracks. Guilt and shame along with self-loathing are very familiar to her. She even justifies them when they arise because of what sees as her many failings. Her ability to love unconditionally is impressive beyond words. Think of Mother Teresa.

The *Real Woman* is compassionate, kind and generous as well. She, however, expects others to be able to take care of themselves except perhaps in some unexpected circumstances. This has given her the opportunity to discover and claim her own needs and wants. She has no trouble setting boundaries based on her schedule and energy level. She expects others to speak up if they need something knowing she will offer support if she can.

She is loving and gives from her fullness but not her depletion. She takes risks, makes mistakes, and then moves on. There is little to no room for guilt. The *Real Woman's* handicap can be the need to do it all for everyone since she has it "all figured out." She has presented herself as having it all together. As a result, there can be a need to live up to the expectations others have put on her to be able to help them fix their problems powerfully and totally in control.

Both styles can do over-responsibility, one does it in humble smiling service while the other does it in a more assertive or no-holds-barred take-charge style. This shows, underneath it all, we are all more alike than not. Only presentation varies. The *Real Woman* is frequently the *Good Girl* who has developed an awareness of herself through EI with the added ability, when healthy, to now make room for herself in her life.

Be aware that Emotional Intelligence refers to a far deeper level of self-awareness and self-understanding than is the norm. With it, you can quickly identify what you are feeling, how you are affecting others, and what lies, if any, you are telling yourself. Lies create illusions which destroy the ability to see anything clearly.

A key point is that EI does require the Mindfulness I talked about earlier. It also takes time, absolute honesty with yourself, and a willingness and degree of patience many don't choose to invest. You need to always be open to learning what causes you to react rather than respond, to feel hurt rather than anger, to feel fear rather than power. It is a choice, you know. Any emotion can come up at any moment in time. The one you choose to stay in is dependent upon you, however. Your ability to be an effective leader requires you to choose which emotions you hold on to. Decades ago, a mentor told me that confusion is a powerful woman's greatest defense. It gives her permission to stay stuck and thus never make a mistake. If you are ever feeling stuck, and stay there, now you know you are in a "safe" place with a high price tag.

Playing stuck or dumb are options a *Real Woman* doesn't have. Women are natural nurturers and this world definitely needs nurturing. Consequently, your leadership needs to be in place now. Movement, action, and change are where progress can be made. If you are going for transformational leadership, such as shifting the world to a better place, it is imperative that you lead with your Emotional Intelligence strongly developed.

You will be dealing with the messages that medicine, business, and politics "are the way they are." As if there is no option for change. "Things have always been done this way." You may even hear "This is how it works." when you know damn well it isn't working.

Before putting someone else's house in order, however, you need to make sure yours is in shape first. Rather than spending time looking at "them", whoever they are, in preparation for your future work, you need to look at yourself. Become a real leader of yourself. It makes you an amazing role model and prepares you for what follows. Begin by recognizing that your life is exactly where you have taken it. Everyone and everything in your life at this moment is there because you allowed it.

You need to take responsibility for every choice you have made, whether or not others encouraged it or went along with it. If your relationships have no intimacy, how much of it do you bring to the table? How willing are you to let that slide? If you are overweight what have you seriously, not half-heartedly, done to change it? Emotional Intelligence allows you to see your truth in each of these situations. It eliminates passivity and brings responsibility back to your doorstep. No blame - just responsibility for change.

If you hate your job, why are you staying? If it is a choice to stay until you find something better, then being there is a choice, so playing victim is a lie. You don't have control over everything that shows up, but you do have control over what you allow to stay. Emotional Intelligence knows that.

If you repeatedly bring in the same types of relationships, the same dramas, the same business difficulties, you need to look at your part in creating them. A *Good Girl* will frequently stay stuck because she is afraid to offer an ultimatum to herself or to others. She is afraid to ask someone else to take responsibility for their life and their choices, their part in the story she or they have created, because she will not want to challenge them. They will blame her anyway and she will readily, even though at times resentfully, take the blame.

Consequently, the *Good Girl* will try to fix the whole story on her own, their part as well as hers. Confrontation is never her strength since she finds it cruel or problematic. There is an old saying "I wish I could, but I can't." It generally means you are not willing to pay the price you would need to pay. The *Good Girl* also means "I don't want THEM to have to pay a price either. I would feel guilty."

The *Good Girl* can be so busy caretaking and problem solving she tells herself she has no time to stop or for any self-care. In reality, others will survive if you take 5 minutes for yourself. They will also like you better afterwards. A non-stressed you is the best you and the easiest to get along with. In addition, you may find they fix their own problems while you are breathing, stopping, and giving them space to do so.

In contrast, the *Real Woman,* once she identifies a problem, will own her role in it and immediately begin to make the changes needed. She will want clean, no-strings-attached solutions. No blame, no victim, no rationalizations, just dealing with what is and finding solutions. The difference is that she will own her part in the problem, but not anyone else's... She will confront others if needed in looking for a mutual resolution if that is possible. Her relationships are far stronger, cleaner, healthier, and mutual because of that skill. Energetically, she feels so much lighter within herself and to be around.

On the road to becoming the *Real Woman*, you will make mistakes, we all do, yet guilt, a *Good Girl* tendency, is a useless emotion that can hold you back on that road. If you make a mistake, admit it and then rectify things as best you can and move on. Becoming a *Real Women* requires it. Becoming a *Real Woman* demands owning what is, not wasting time wishing things were different.

One great benefit of developed Emotional Intelligence for everyone is the letting go of illusions such as victim and powerless. Releasing blame, guilt, shame, and so on, allows you to finally be the real you.

Not the perfect you; she doesn't exist, but the you who makes mistakes and who learns from them.

Honestly, freedom, empowerment, personal responsibility, and self-appreciation increases daily when increasing your Emotional Intelligence becomes a way of life. A great benefit is that the *Good Girl* can't exist in that world, so she ceases to be a central part of your life. She begins to disappear. You may fall back there on occasion but only briefly. Being emotionally intelligent with yourself is how you become free from her clutches and tendencies.

Another gift of Emotional Intelligence is knowing when you are stressed and not taking it out on others. It is your responsibility to own it and do self-care. Walk, mediate, breathe, change the situation any way you choose. Call a friend or watch a funny video.

My default when I start to feel overwhelmed or depressed is *Mama Mia*. I have 2 copies. Ten minutes in and I am back, singing and swaying with the crowd and grateful to be alive. Find yours. Breathe. Even in the midst of a meeting. Disengage for a moment and breathe. I close my eyes and go into the Caribbean Sea for a quick dip. I love that water, so I am chillin'.

The *Real Woman* knows the difference it makes and stops, without guilt. She recognizes the world can survive without her for a few moments, even a few hours.

She's real and her inner peace, her being centered, is what allows her to keep things in perspective and she knows she needs that. Having permission from yourself to develop this level of Emotional Intelligence, to know yourself and your emotions so well, and what they need for balance, is the key to radical self-confidence and self-love. Plus you will never have too much of either.

For added support know that Emotional Intelligence:

- Allows change to happen – even encourages it

- Doesn't take things personally

- Doesn't expect perfection from self or others

- Helps you understand why and when you react versus respond

- Confronts problems not people - readily and without conflict

- Sets boundaries

- Knows when to stay and when to walk away.

Just think, by this point Mindset, Communication Skills, Mindfulness, and Emotional Intelligence are yours. You got this!

GETTING REAL:

1. How much time, if any, do you spend daily in developing your EI?

2. Have you developed the ability to step out of a situation and assess whether you are responding or reacting?

3. Have you developed the ability to see someone else's responsibility without doing blame?

4. Do you need to have all the answers to feel safe?

5. Can you see the difference between feeling passion and emotion?

CHAPTER FIVE

BECOMING THE HERO

Meeting them where they are.

When you are successful, or at least appear to be, others get impressions of you, you never could have imagined. At times people need a hero, and in all humility, you may need to step up to the plate.

They may see something in you they want to believe is possible for them. Your gift to them can be to permit it, temporarily…

One of the businesses I have founded was an institute, the Institute of Healing Arts and Sciences. It offered 2-and 4-year programs in a method of Energy Medicine I had developed. The W.I.S.E. Method (wholistic, integrated, spiritual, energies.)

There was a significant emphasis on personal growth since I don't believe you can be an effective healer until you have done your own healing. In addition, each weekend they learned a new healing technique I had developed in resolving various diseases and disorders.

I soon became known as the "Dottie Lama," a name a student created that quickly caught on and lasted for 19 years. I was initially embarrassed beyond words but soon could find humor and purpose in it as well. You can imagine the impression it made, however, each year as the new group of first year students showed up.

For example, one day as a friend and I were walking down the hall during a break, a new student approached and asked if she could touch me. Thinking a label was sticking out or something, I said "Sure, thanks." Instead this woman touched my arm and turned to her friend and said, "I touched her." as they walked away.

My girlfriend and I walked outside and just looked at each other speechless. Finally, she smiled and said, "She needs you to be her strength for a bit." To this day I remember that odd and surreal feeling as well as the realization that my girlfriend was correct.

I knew as founder it was my job to support students in seeing that what they project onto others is what they also value in themselves. What would the *Good Girl* do in this situation? *The Good Girl* would likely never even discuss it for fear of seeming egotistical or making the woman feel uncomfortable.

What about the *Real Woman*? She recognizes that at times we all need to see someone, some human as greater than ourselves. We need to know something more is possible, and the *Real Woman* is willing to fill that role temporarily if needed.

I chose to teach about the need to recognize our own gifts and to acknowledge that we are drawn to traits in others that we already possess. I pointed out hers, so she could begin to see what I saw.

When you become the *Real Woman,* others who haven't seen themselves that way yet may need you to be their benchmark. They may need to see you as their mentor directly or indirectly. As your gift to them, you may need to let them see you in that light.

It certainly puts pressure on you to recognize your responsibility to be that *Real Woman* and not collapse into illusion or fear. In that instance, they are a gift to you as well. They call you to stand in the truth of who you are, a place you want to be in. Over time, as they see your many strengths and you become more comfortable owning them, they will also see your humanity.

The world needs leaders; and it needs heroes, or heroines. It needs to believe there is hope, that there is possibility. We can each provide that if we are willing. In my work, I bring the message that anything is possible. I want to inspire and call others to go after their "impossible" just because they can. As Linda Ronstadt says: "The impossible just takes a little longer."

The important factor for the chosen heroine is to always stay the *Real Woman.* Do not go into ego, delusions of grandeur, or self-betrayal since they quickly take you away from the gift of your realness. In doing so, you become a false hero rather than a help.

If you currently recognize yourself as the *Good Girl* know that you can grow into the *Real Woman,* if you choose. She is already there hidden beneath the desire to please the world in order to be loved or "good enough." You already are. You will be qualified to be there as a *Real Woman,* on your own, when you are willing to give up the illusion of being the great savior of all those in need. As the *Good Girl* you need to be needed so you have taught everyone to rely on you. Can you give that up? Who will you will be without that role?

That's a frightening question to ask. How do you give up the image, the persona, of who you thought you were supposed to be, who you have spent your life trying to become? As you begin to question the value of your stance, you need to see options. As the *Real Woman* you can be that beacon, that option she can reach for, for herself. You become that hero, that one who she believes has made it without any difficulties.

You become the one the *Good Girl* now wants to be. It's only as she moves into her own inner reality, away from that struggle for perfection through service, empathy, thoughtfulness, and self-sacrifice that she begins to recognize your humanity as well. At that point, she is developing the strength to stand on her own. Your role as hero was a gift when she needed it and now it can end. You, however, must let it go.

When the *Good Girl* struggled to achieve an ideal, perhaps perfection or being all-loving, which isn't real, and which certainly wasn't who she was, she got lost. Her way back is in letting herself be human, be real, and to feel. I know for myself, after spending a decade trying to be the perfect *Good Girl,* the perfect wife, the perfect mother, the perfect neighbor, and on and on, and on, one day I finally realized I couldn't do it and I didn't want to. I recognized that I was absolutely depressed and depleted.

Surprisingly perhaps, I was thrilled to feel depressed. I was finally feeling. I didn't care what the feeling was. I felt. It was my point of beginning my way back into the world, my beginning back into me. It was as if a dam broke. I quickly decided to go back to school to get a graduate degree. I decided I was going to start a career once I graduated as a psychotherapist. I had a plan. More importantly, I had a life.

We all play the *Good Girl* role on occasion. Some as a way of life, some for a period of our life, and for others still, we default into it in particular situations. Let go of blame, judgment, or self-hatred. You are a product of your upbringing and your experiences. Recognize you betray yourself to be that "perfect" *Good Girl* you were taught you should be. The *Real Woman* goes there rarely but it also makes her real, human, and approachable for those who see her as their role model, their mentor, or their hero.

You can't ask for the hero position. That is artificial, and ego based, a defensive move to prove your worth. Rather, what makes you real is your commitment to be the best you, you can be. You may take years working to know who you are, and how you get in your own way, through using Mindfulness and Emotional Intelligence. Know it is worth the effort.

The *Good Girl* isn't bad, and the *Real Woman* isn't a saint. They are both human beings trying to be everything they are capable of. The differentiator is that the *Good Girl* is following everything others expect of her while the *Real Woman* is respecting her own inner calling and working to become her best self by following the messages from her own heart and her soul. Both are good people, but one has aged into adulthood and independence and is now ready to soar as high as her dreams can carry her!

GETTING REAL:

1. Can you see yourself as a hero?

2. Have you ever had someone you looked up to in that way?

3. Can you balance humility with being powerful and leading?

4. Is the *Good Girl* keeping you in "support" rather than "leader" mode?

5. Can you energetically feel the difference between those two modes?

CHAPTER SIX

OUR SHADOW SIDE

Yes, it does exist.

Let's take a short walk to the other side of the tracks, to that part of you, you may want to deny exists. Each of these ladies, the *Good Girl* and the *Real Woman* has a darker side where she allows all of her anger, frustration, and vulnerabilities to show. It's not necessarily pretty but it is certainly real, for each of them.

Your shadow side, dark side, or lower self, whatever you may call it, is not evil, bad, or worthy of condemnation. It is simply that part of yourself you are in conflict with. Looking at it, bringing it into the light, may allow you to see it for what it is. Its function is to keep you alive and safe, even if it does so in pretty self-destructive ways.

Your shadow emerges when you are feeling frightened, vulnerable, angry, hate-filled, and so forth - feelings that you may be too embarrassed to acknowledge. They are against all the images of yourself you want to believe.

They are also perfectly normal. When the *Good Girl* gives endlessly, selflessly, for hours if not days on end, doesn't it make sense that at some point she will feel resentment, anger, or even hatred? When her life doesn't look anything like she imagined doesn't it make sense that she will wonder what on earth she was thinking? When her relationship seems like one exhausting power-struggle after another doesn't it make sense she would want to be single again even for a few minutes? Welcome to normalcy and welcome to humanity.

Every mother I know has this image of her children adoring her while she is the mother who adores them every moment, loving them unconditionally. Yet if she is honest, hasn't she also said a least a dozen times (sometimes in a day) that she doesn't know what she was thinking? There are moments, she doesn't like her kids or know if she even wants to be a mother anymore. When my kids were teenagers, and I was exhausted from the demands or arguments, I would say "I'm going to sell you for a nickel to the first taker!" Amy would say "Mom, you'd be chasing the car down the driveway; that threat doesn't work with us."

I was thrilled they knew they were adored but they also knew I had nothing left to give at that moment. It was time for them to chill. Holding everything in for fear they were too fragile to know I was exhausted was ridiculous. People know how you feel without your saying a word, especially your kids. Resentment, sarcasm, passive aggressiveness, illusions of victimization, cruelty, powerlessness, and murderous rage are all parts of the *Good Girl's* shadow. This is where the strength of her raw emotions gets played out. This is where her power and passion are most felt. Otherwise, she would be totally and tightly containing everything, except her anxiety, with no outlet.

When she has had enough, for a short period of time she gets to play the abused peasant turned avenger, going after all the enemies who have brutalized her for the past 3-6 months. Her ability to remember every slight is astounding. She will rant and rave and terrify the entire house for an hour or two perhaps, and then collapse.

Because she isn't used to venting so aggressively, so powerfully, her system can't maintain it for too long. For a brief period, she feels amazing now that all that pent-up emotion has been released. She is free and clear, no energy blockages left. Life is good.

She was the hero who saved the day and put all the enemies, the users, and abusers in their place. As you can expect, the exultation is also short-lived. Guilt, compassion, and her normal behavior returns when everyone comes out of hiding. She now gets to reclaim her status as a martyr.

Unfortunately, she hasn't resolved anything. She hasn't confronted the issues, or, established new behavior patterns for herself or those around her. She only dumped and ran. Nothing will change since the parents or the mom have decided that this is the dance they will do in this house. Everyone knows their steps. Life is perfect. It's what the *Good Girl* learned as a child.

Although the *Real Woman* can briefly visit the martyr/avenger role on occasion, she has a very different shadow style. She has claimed her power as a daily occurrence. However, when she is exhausted or angry she can readily use her honesty and openness as cruel and abusive weapons. Having it "all together" can create quite a sense of righteousness, superiority, and detachment. Through her shadow side, she gets to express every one of them. She is "above" the daily hassles of living and wants the "peasantry" to know that.

When she is hurt, wounded, or angry she can easily forget all that she learned through Mindfulness as well as lose touch with her Emotional Intelligence and she can then become immensely intimidating. She becomes the wounded warrior on the attack. She can make anyone feel small and love doing it. She will righteously put everyone and anyone "in their place." As if she knew where that was...

She can readily cut people off or take charge even when her domination isn't wanted. She will, nonetheless, be offended when her "help" isn't valued or appreciated and will take that rejection as a personal insult. She will cut you off as if you never existed because she is feeling so hurt and rejected. You will experience her as being short, abrasive, and a force to be reckoned with.

Simultaneously, I frequently see that when the *Real Woman* is overwhelmed the little girl comes out. This vulnerable little girl, who just wants to be loved and nurtured. It is such a touching site. However, because she is also frightening, you have no idea when the attacker will show up and reign because her erratic emotions are running the show. It is as if the burden of having it all together is too exhausting, and she just wants a break to be human, to be a cherished child, or simply a woman comfortable just being.

When having it altogether is slipping and she isn't comfortable admitting it, the *Real Woman* may also go into self-betrayal by pretending everything is fine and wearing the mask or persona of success, order, and power. It protects her vulnerability while terrifying her.

Whether you are in the role of *Good Girl* or *Real Woman*, when you slip to your shadow side, you can avoid the rants, the cruelty, and other acts of self-betrayal, by being honest, being real, and admitting it to yourself and the others.

For the *Good Girl,* give until you are tired not exhausted. For the *Real Woman* know you generally have it all together but in being human there are moments, when you just wake up feeling inadequate, or unloved, or lost in the chaos of success and you just want to suck your thumb and stay in bed. Both of you can do so…

The practice of Mindfulness, living fully in the moment, lets you know when you can't hold it together or hold it up any longer. At that moment, your developed Emotional Intelligence knows you need to stop or pull back. "Just one more" is the killer. It is the ice on the walkway. Avoid the desire to keep pushing. There is always a price to pay when you bargain with yourself. Not only will you risk sliding into shadow behavior, you also risk making careless mistakes you never would have made otherwise.

Delightfully, I have found that just before you need to go into "force mode" taking a 15-minute break to change your scenery, your energy, or your situation, may be all that is needed.

For those times when it isn't, or when it never crosses your mind to stop and pull it together, you need to accept that the shadow takes over when you are exhausted. Sleep may be the main requirement but perhaps a lite dinner, a glass of wine, or a movie and then early to bed are a requirement and something to look forward to at the end of the day to provide much needed self-nurturance. Just think about it.

Now I'm going to discuss a topic that is rarely discussed in "public," especially in a book discussing spiritual and realistic leadership - having an affair. Statistically women are cheating in far greater numbers than ever before and where else but in the shadow side would it live?

Data from the General Social Survey shows that millennial women are cheating more than millennial men. It is not the numbers or the percentages that are important to me here nor am I judging women who cheat. I am focused far more on you living in your truth, your integrity, and your sense of self.

If the *Real Woman* is going to be real, and the *Good Girl* is going to be good then where does cheating fit? In both places - because affairs take place for any number of reasons.

The *Good Girl* can feel invisible in a marriage where she frequently feels completely apart from, or secondary to, her partner's world. She may believe her partner takes advantage of her and so she wants to act out and be appreciated by someone, anyone. She may also want to have something that is just hers.

The *Real Woman* may feel that she is tired of being in the Alpha role and wants to feel feminine, light, free, completely unburdened, and to let someone take care of her for a change. It is as if she is on vacation from her life, from the responsibilities of work, family and even extended family if she has elderly parents.

Affairs can make you feel alive, passionate, and wanted. Most importantly, they can make you fall in love with the woman you want to be or remind you after a long break away that she still exists. She is passionate, uninhibited, alive, and so ready to break free. She is the primary woman you love, have forgotten, or perhaps never knew.

In my work as a psychotherapist and coach I have heard it all. Some say they cheat for the sex since they love their husbands but his sex drive is gone, and masturbation isn't sufficient. Some say they cheat because he does it too. Most simply say, "It just happened." and it makes them feel alive. Nothing "just happens" and sadly, for them, the only way to feel alive is hidden in the shadows.

My focus here is to support you as you let the *Good Girl* die and become the *Real Woman* you are called to be - a woman with her head held high - owning all of who she is.

Fearing your secrets will be discovered will only weigh you down. Why put a marriage you want in jeopardy? If your marriage truly doesn't work, why are you in it? What are you frightened of losing if you left? Does the cost of safety mean losing yourself?

In addition, most relationships begun within an affair do not last and guess who tends to get devastated? The pain is enormous and who can you talk to about it? How can you take time off to grieve a secret when you have a job and a family with so many demands?

Both the *Good Girl* and the *Real Woman* need to know that deception leads to guilt and self-hatred. Then comes depression and that impacts every element of your life. It calls you to disassociate from all those parts of you that you are discovering through Mindfulness and Emotional Intelligence. Ultimately, the price of an affair can be way too high.

Take the best part of it and fall in love with yourself all over again. Fall in love with the woman and the life you are creating. Fall in love with your unlimited potential. We all deserve to be in love, and to have our sexual needs met, just stay in love with yourself in the process.

Bring that new you into your relationship; it may surprise you what happens. One client said to me, "For thirty-five years I thought he was the ass----. I just realized I was – and now my marriage is brand new. I love it. Who knew?"

More than once I have seen a one-time, short-term affair make a marriage better than ever before. Frequently what was happening was that the being in love was being replaced with responsibilities, demands on time, and feeling lost in the relationship and in life. It wasn't even about the partner. The short-term affair woke him or her up and showed them the type of relationship they wanted. What they did was realize they wanted it with their spouse, so they took the experience of coming alive back into their marriage and transformed it. They had tools and experience now to create the marriage they never knew they wanted, and it was far better than ever before. I am not advocating an affair simply saying that if you have had one did you use it to weaken, destroy, or strengthen your marriage?

If you need to leave and had an affair to give you the strength to get out, do so but leave because of where you are or where your partner is; leave because it cannot be saved, or perhaps never should have happened. Do not leave because of someone else, who, for the moment, seems near-perfect. Rarely, does a partner in an affair become a spouse. If he or she does, it is even rarer that it lasts. Don't get lost in illusion.

Remember that your shadow creates situations because of primal need. It is your fear, sadness, or anger trying to protect you. Your fear is ready to attack a perceived enemy, your sadness is trying to prove you are worthy, and your anger is getting back at the bad guys. Unfortunately, the biggest result is your own self-destruction and a resultant increase in your self-hatred. It doesn't support self-love only a need for survival.

Recognize it for what it does. It searches for safety regardless of the cost and regardless of what it takes. It searches for love from a wounded and rejected place. It searches for acceptance from outside. It is the wounded self, searching for what it believes it does not have. It is not the enemy. It is a child that needs to be acknowledged but it should never have control.

It is in the shadows that self-betrayal takes place. Recognize the messages and use your Emotional Intelligence and Mindfulness, or friends, a coach, whatever you need to keep from handing over control. Most importantly, learn to laugh at this side of you that hopefully never goes away. Really!

She is the outrageous side you want to share with a friend when you know you need 15 minutes to swear like a trooper, condemn everyone you know, put everyone down, ridicule the world, and then, when spent, collapse and laugh with the ones you trust. They are the ones who know and accept your shadow side. They watch it pop up where no one gets hurt, including you. They love the passion, the outrageousness, and that side of you, you rarely show. They may even encourage her to come out further in this safe, love-filled place. Let her. Learn to love feeling alive just do not let her hurt you. It is only energy and energy is never good or bad. Just use it constructively, not destructively, on yourself or another.

When you are done, allow your Emotional Intelligence to recognize the cost of taking this outside to a crowd and choose your higher self. It brings far more joy, allows you to stop the tirade, or the affair, or anything else before it controls you rather than you controlling it. If you can't, accept your humanity, come back to your truth when you can, and know this is a journey, of loving, holy souls growing and learning. You will never be "perfect" whatever that is, but you will always be amazing and on a journey you never could have predicted and, sometimes, learning your lessons the hardest way possible…

GETTING REAL:

1. How do you identify your shadow side?

2. Can you identify it when it first shows up?

3. How destructive do you let it get?

4. Do you waste time justifying it?

5. Can you channel that to creative energy to make your world a better place?

CHAPTER SEVEN

COLLABORATION

Choosing power - eliminating competition!

Collaboration is described as the art of working jointly with others. For most women this is purely instinctive. As nurturers and multi-taskers, working with others is a well-developed skill we generally bring into all of our group interactions, especially the workplace.

The women of the senate used this gift when they ended the 2013 government shutdown after their male colleagues weren't able to do so. The men showed that going for the win was ineffective as it is in most every situation. When one person wins and another loses, the relationship always suffers. Holding a point of view simply to prove you can becomes a display of ego over all else.

To a limited extent, combative competition may belong on the sports field where it frequently encourages competitors to do their best. Even there, however, we have many examples where collaboration with heart fits far more than combative competition and has world-wide impact. At the 2016 Olympics two women had collided after one fell, and more than once each stopped to help the other up, resulting in each woman coming in last together, yet they inspired the world.

https://www.theguardian.com/sport/2016/aug/17/olympic-spirit-new-zealand-and-american-runners-help-each-other-after-collision

Even in World War 1, German, French, and English soldiers chose to cease fire on Christmas day, walk out of their trenches, and sing Christmas carols together, playing soccer, and smoking cigarettes. The "enemy" is often a mirror of us beneath it all. Collaborating for one day in the midst of hell was a gift they gave each other.

https://www.history.com/news/world-war-is-christmas-truce-100-years-ago

Anyone can collaborate, yet the first example presented was viewed as exceptional sportsmanship by women. The second example was a shocking awareness that even on what would be the death bed of some, collaboration with "the enemy" was far more palatable than destructive competition.

Collaboration doesn't just happen unless it's your normal style. There are necessary agreements that have to be in place for it to work:

1. Having clear definitions of the roles for each partner

2. Open communication to share the information necessary

3. Consensus about goals and projects or tasks

4. Recognition of, and respect for, the contributions from everyone

5. Identifying and addressing obstacles and problems

6. Group goals are placed over personal satisfaction

7. Willingness to apologize for mistakes and the ability to forgive others.

The women senators' willingness to put egos, the illusion of each side having the one right answer, and the need to win, aside, actually resulted in so much more than just winning. They united to solve a problem and everyone came out ahead in solving a theoretically "unsolvable" problem. You can be assured, each of the steps above were followed. The men will tell you, quite humbly and honestly, that the women ended the stand-off that they could not.

The women did not make everything perfect for everyone; they did not make everyone good friends. What they did, however, was find a compromise that was acceptable to each group. Isn't that what learning how to work together is about? Collaboration? They created a win-win situation which was so much bigger than just the people in the room...

Collaboration, our strength, needs to be a valued skill we use to support one another as well as the organizations where we work. Too frequently, women work against each other. If we are going to support the bigger vision of having more women in medicine, business, and politics, we need to help each other every step of the way. When there is a woman who you know would be perfect for a job, what are you doing to help her get it? Are there tips you could offer to her? Are there people you could introduce her to? Is there a meeting or conference she should know about?

Walking through life as a collaborator changes your perspective and it changes your potential. It changes how you face problems in the office or at home. It supports you in taking responsibility for what is yours without the need to take on responsibilities that belong to others. It also lets you see that you are a significant addition to any team, where you listen to others in addition to sharing your thoughts. You support others, yes, but you do not carry them. They are your peers, or your mentors, but never your responsibility.

Not coincidentally, as I am writing this, I just got a text from a friend who has referred me to someone who was looking for a speaker on leadership. She asks for one vodka gimlet as payment. That is a friend and ally since of course I will need to have a gimlet with her....

That is such a contrast to a situation a client recently spoke about. She had applied for a position with a new company and found out later that the woman she interviewed with, who would have been her peer, felt my client was too powerful and too smart and thus voted against hiring her. This would have been an amazing opportunity for my client as well as for the other women to learn from each other, instead both lost out.

Along with these self-created difficulties, women are still facing a gender bias. Certainly not all men are biased but it is a significant enough number that we need to support each other in working through these biases until they are non-existent. The glass ceiling may be cracking but it is still there. It may be that individual women, with support from others, are what will destroy this ceiling one board position or one CEO, COO or CFO spot at a time. If so, it will be so much more efficient if we do it together. This is a *Real Woman* task. She is the one who will change the world. When we work in unison, in collaboration, there will be no stopping her or us!

Seeing each other as allies rather than competitors, as sisters rather than enemies, as mentors, as partners and so forth allows each of us to win. When I hear of a conference coming up I submit a proposal to speak and then notify friends who may also be a great fit, so they can apply as well. It supports their income or their circle of influence or both. We are all in this together and sharing our resources is an easy gift to give. It costs you nothing yet gets you so much.

In expanding on this, while seeing herself within the big picture, the *Real Woman* is aware of her skills as well as her need to continue growing and she knows she can learn a great deal from those who have gone before her. They are those who may have made mistakes she can avoid. They are the ones who have learned an easier way to approach a certain problem or person. Sharing in their wisdom, with a willingness to learn from them, makes us perfect collaborators, supports, and gifts to each other.

Mentors are free and can guide you along the path you want to go because they have walked it before you. Other forms of collaborators are coaches who you pay. They come in many forms. Some coaches are very specific in focus such as accounting, marketing, or social media. Others are more expansive in their offerings, supporting you in developing leadership skills, while working with you to see the ways in which you self-sabotage within various meetings and initiatives, perhaps also calling you to expand your skills and career potential.

Over time you learn what you need and what you have to offer as others ask you to be their mentor. I can share with you that just as a teacher conquers the subject matter through teaching, a mentor solidifies their knowledge, wisdom, and skills through their mentoring. You recognize you know far more than you realized. You become far more confident as you see the big picture as well as the details and perspectives you are sharing. Within collaboration, everyone wins.

The need to be collaborative is applicable whether you are the security guard at the front desk or the CEO on the 21st floor. Learning to work in collaboration with other women makes working in collaboration with anyone a much more natural process. Over time, you learn to see the strengths everyone can bring to the table even if they are dramatically different from your own.

You will be setting up a pattern of constant win-win for yourself. That is a really smart move no matter what your goals are. You never know when you may need to restart a government and of course you want to be ready...

GETTING REAL:

1. Do you need to win at all costs?

2. Does collaboration seem like a losing proposition?

3. Do you have experience in asking others to work with you to find a better solution whether in brainstorming or mentoring?

4. Have you ever worked with a coach?

5. Should you? What would the benefits be?

CHAPTER EIGHT

RELATIONSHIPS

We make them what we envision.

For most all of us, depending upon the day, relationships of any kind are both a blessing and a curse. They are a gift beyond words and yet they call you to become your best self even when you don't want to talk to anyone. Without relationships however, life is so much emptier with far less laughter, love, hope, and dreams.

A quick overview:

Most frequently, our first relationships are with our parents. Our mothers taught us how to be women, and our dads taught us what to expect from men. That is where the "fun" begins…

We had human parents who could only teach us what they knew. As you are well aware, some knew very little. Some knew a fair amount. Generally speaking, we can say, and I say this as a parent myself, they could only do their best.

In trying to adapt to our family, we learned early what worked. Children are so amazingly intuitive, instinctive, and aware, usually far more than parents could ever imagine. Each child found what worked for him or her. In the same family there can be any number of adaptive styles.

Standard teaching in understanding alcoholic systems, (which also applies in most family systems, so I am sharing it) is that:

- One child zones out by reading ferociously.

- One child acts out frequently

- One child becomes the appeaser trying to make everyone happy

- One child becomes "perfect" to distance from any problems

- One child finds many friends to avoid uncomfortable situations in the house.

None of these coping mechanisms is wrong. Children learn to live, and hopefully thrive, within their family in their own unique way. The challenge is that, as adults, frequently the style we chose as children no longer works and even becomes detrimental rather than supportive and adaptive for us as adults. The bigger world is not your family and therefore your old ways of being may no longer support your development or your potential for success.

When you haven't yet developed sufficient EI to understand your own behavior and belief systems or to recognize that they are primarily a byproduct of your upbringing, you believe they are universal. You believe everyone thinks and feels the way you do (or that everyone is revolting against the same rules that you are.) It wasn't until I was 22 that I met someone who didn't eat fish on Fridays. I thought the whole world did. It was a universal rule according to my teachings.

It wasn't until I left the convent and moved to New York City three months later as an international airline stewardess that I met my first career woman. It was also the first time I ever heard people say others have the right to live any life style they chose. There was freedom everywhere and all I knew at that moment was that I didn't fit in. I had no idea how to process all the new realties being presented. I was told as an international stewardess that the pilots were married in the states but we were working in Paris so the rules were different. (I was told that by pilots of course....)

I truly had no idea in that moment what was right or wrong, what was truth and what wasn't. Because of a lack of exposure most of us are not prepared for the reality that many approaches to life are right, not just one or that many lifestyles are healthy, not just ours. It was during that period that I first knew I needed to look within. I had to look at me in the mirror each day and I had to define for me what my values, world views, and behaviors would be. I no longer wanted to be a *Good Girl,* but I had absolutely no idea how to be a *Real Woman.*

Like most, consciously, or unconsciously, as a result of so much coming at me, for safety or predictability I initially worked to create a world that functioned according to the dynamics I learned as a child, only better. It would feel familiar and I would fit in. This is why although many women after having broken free from oppressive homes, nonetheless marry people who want total control over them. If your father or mother was physically abusive you may feel a partner who is only emotionally and spiritually abusive to be light years better than your past. What else do you have to compare it to?

Since you may have learned early that acting or being a certain way caused people to praise you and reward you, you may now think you understand relationship dynamics. Whatever you chose early on it worked for you, even if only to a small degree. Like myself, who initially did *Good Girl* but soon dropped it for attempts at being the *Real Woman,* when we don't have role models we can easily slip back into the *Good Girl* because of the people we bring into our life. Learning Real Woman on our own requires practice, failing, coming back, and trying again until it becomes our home base.

What I discovered as a psychotherapist in private practice, seeing 42 patients a week, and as a teacher and coach, is that the *Good Girl* frequently grew up in a home that had a dominant parent demanding obedience. There were very strict guidelines for who a girl should be with very defined rules, regulations, and restrictions.

Sometimes the *Good Girl* grew up in a home that was also violent and chaotic so that being "good" was her way of minimizing the craziness and unpredictability of her life at home and elsewhere. Finally, for some, it was a way of modeling what she thought was how the "nice" families or "successful" families did it. Religions and our social culture certainly had an additional role in that as well, teaching us to be seen and not heard. On occasion, a *Real Woman* may have been blessed with a home in which the children were cherished, guided, and shown discipline, but cherished was the key so she saw her intrinsic worth early.

Whatever the dynamic in your early years, recognize and understand it, but know that your patterns of relationship as an adult are the result of the decisions you alone have made. Yes, we all learned how to do relationships from our parents by observing their relationships with each other and with others. That created the blueprint – but only the blueprint - for your future. You decided whether or not to keep it as it was or to change it.

Examples I have used to explain this are:

Your parents told you:

- Not to eat before meals, yet do you now eat appetizers when out networking etc.?
- Not to talk to strangers yet I bet you do it daily
- To always wear coats in cold weather yet now you "run out" frequently
- To always wear raincoats if it is going to rain that day – really?
- Never kiss on the first date
- Never have sex until after marriage
- To "clean your plate" at meals
- Never interrupt
- Never speak with your mouth full

They also said:

- "You'll never learn."

- "You never listen."

- "You'll never be good enough."

From these lists and elsewhere, how many past messages have you maintained? In truth, you dropped the ones that no longer fit or that you no longer wanted, and you kept the rest. Why? Because it suited you. You kept the ones that matched the self-image you chose to maintain whether it was the best for you or not.

Without self-judgment or blame take responsibility for the messages you kept as well as the ones you dropped. You can no longer blame your parents for whatever messages you chose to keep. Whether you expanded some, changed them, or threw them out, it has been your choice all along and most certainly your choice since you left high school. Too many remain in the child state, still blaming their parents for their recurring behavior and their beliefs.

The gift of Mindfulness and EI is that you can begin to see which of the behaviors and beliefs you profess to accept truly reflect who you are or who you want to become. In workshops I ask participants to write down expressions - without judgement - that they say frequently and then ask them to verify the truth of each one. Standardly, there is shock when they realize they blindly say expressions they have learned but as they actually listen to them they don't believe some at all. It's time then to rethink what is said and see if it reflects the woman you want to be.

A message my father gave me was that if you are from the housing projects you belong in the projects as long as you live. It is your home and to leave is to betray "your people." I have owned a few homes, each progressively larger than the last and not one was in Massachusetts much less Boston. I have also lived on the Caribbean island of Anguilla, BWI for 10 years. Although I still described myself as from South Boston, which pleased my father, the truth, however, was every morning in Anguilla as I walked into the water of the Caribbean, I was close to tears and in awe thinking "this is my home." I grew up in South Boston but Anguilla was home.

This is not an innocent statement. I could carry myself as a girl from the projects of South Boston or I could carry myself as the founder of 4 companies and an international speaker living in Anguilla. The energetic ownership defined so much from the moment people met me. Who were they going to see? This was about my relationship with me. Who did I identify with? Notice what you say; is it truth? You hear your own words and they have impact on you.

The same is applicable to your relationships. Once you were old enough to be exposed to different types of friends or partners you became aware of options. Are you with someone you continuously complain about? Why do you need to do relationships that way? He or she is not perfect, no one is. Why do you choose to focus on the negative? On the opposite position, if a great deal is wrong, unhealthy, and even dangerous, do you need to see only the good, practicing avoidance so that you can stay? Where did you learn to do that? From whom?

In looking at your relationships with others:

- How do you do relationships now?
- What kind of partner/partners have you brought in?
- What kinds of friendships do you have?
- Do you have friendships or just acquaintances?
- Are you invisible?
- Are you loved and cherished by anyone? One Person? Many?

What have you learned, if anything, from past relationships? When a relationship ends, whether with a friend or a lover, do you take time to learn whatever lessons there are to learn from it? Do you play victim and blame the other person for all the things that didn't work? Can you, without judgement, learn from this relationship things about yourself? About how you do relationships?

I personally look at why I picked this person in the first place. Was I simply lonely? Were there warning signs I didn't want to see? What in me found him attractive? Why did I stay as long as I did? What did I learn about what I do or don't do in relationship? What did I learn about what I say or don't say? Did I betray myself a lot? Did it simply end because we are in different places in our lives and I still think he is terrific but not for me? What can I learn so that next time I am wiser about my choices in terms of what is right for me (not what is wrong with him/her.)? What have I learned from this gift of loving and being loved?

Whatever you discover from these questions is in your power to improve upon, keep as it is, or change. All the options are yours. Think of the power you possess...... A saying of mine fits perfectly here: "Life is simple, it just isn't always easy." What I mean by that is, if there is something you don't like, change it. Period. Simple. If you don't want to change it, accept it and stop complaining.

If you do want to change it but no one else does, leave… Simple, but not always easy. The most important element here is that it is your choice……. No blame, no victim, no powerlessness, and no accusations. Just choice. You are the leader and creator of this life you are living. You have absolutely no ability to change someone else so let that illusion go. If you need them to change to suit you, you are not really in love with them in the first place and a useless battle will go nowhere.

Not surprisingly, the *Good Girl* is prone to entering two types of relationships. In the first type, she longs to be with someone who holds her up as his "everything." In this she is easily manipulated, seduced, and cherished. She feels as if she has won the jackpot. Eventually, enmeshment, co-dependency, and her neediness to be loved, becomes suffocating. Her partner starts fighting for space or simply pulls back. This fills her with terror of being abandoned and/

or unloved, and unlovable. The fear causes her to hold on tighter and a cycle of abuse or close/apart begins. This gives her partner permission to be in the relationship but not. Something he or she learned in their family of origin.

In the second common style of relationship for the *Good Girl,* she falls in love with someone she can "help." She is absolutely in love with one aspect of her lover's personality yet the other aspect is one she will "help" with. It is often someone she sees who is in pain and who she believes needs her to love him/her enough so that they will be happy and at peace with themselves and the world. In her vision, she will then be cherished beyond words because of how unconditionally loving she was while she healed her partner into this happy, loving, individual.

If you "need" them to change anything, you are not really in love with that person. You are in love with who you want them to be. That is absolutely a betrayal of who they are. When they don't live up to who you wanted to make them into, you say they betrayed you. In fact, you betrayed them. You said, "I love you" and what you really meant was "I love the person I can create from the raw material you have provided. I love your potential and you will develop it whether you want to or not because I demand and expect it. If you don't, you never really loved me enough."

Notice as well that in this relationship the sole focus is your partner. Frequently this partner is very charming initially, smooth, appearing confident, and in control. Only after time is there the realization that adjectives such as controlling, needy, and demanding are more accurate. It is as if you are raising a child. You may even say "S/he is like a child." Really? Or is that the dynamic you brought into this relationship and that s/he went along with? I can assure you that it will end with either you being exhausted and angry at their narcissism and your invisibility or they will end it when they finally realize they are tired of trying to be this person you are demanding they become.

In addition, the *Good Girl* is prone to find others, not just partners, who are very needy. Because she is naturally so unconditionally loving she brings in everyone who is searching to be rescued. If this is you, you never get a break because you have taught them to need you. You have taught them you are available 24/7 and they believed you. You cannot give without ending even to children you adore. You cannot be available 24-7 to anyone and still be refreshed, happy, and at peace. This approach doesn't show your goodness only your unlimited availability.

It is as if you are a magnet for the needy and dependent folks. It is actually quite exhausting. Again, if this is you, where and when do you get your needs met? I am not talking about on your birthday, when you probably end up cleaning up the mess afterwards anyway. When do you allow someone to fill your needs? Can you comfortably accept being catered to? Can you receive with delight and abandon, or do you feel guilty and shameful because they spent so much money or time on you?

Notice if you are usually the one who, when no one else volunteers, does so, reluctantly or otherwise. Notice if by the time it's time for you to do something for yourself you are so exhausted you just go to bed. Finally, see if you can remember the last time you went away with friends to just chill, dance, have a drink, and do nothing? Last month? Last year? Five years ago? Just asking…

The old illusion of "If I don't do it no one will." is the road to insanity. If no one else will do it, it doesn't need to get done. The issue becomes: how can you model healthy self-care, healthy relationships, and a healthy lifestyle to all you are in relationship with? Only by living it! Because of conditioning and a self-image that confuses kind and compassionate with all-giving, you may be giving yourself away at an unhealthy level. Because you are naturally loving, you instinctively want to support others. Do so, but in balance.

The loving traits you possess in caring for others are gifts to those you are with. Those traits, however, are only a small part of who you are. Your dreams, your wants, your ideas, your interests, your skills, and your personality are all traits that when combined define who you are as a woman. In addition, the specific energy you bring into a room when you feel rested, alive, and passionate reflects who you are. It has absolutely nothing to do with giving or supporting others. It is totally just you being your authentic and full self. Giving and doing has nothing to do with it. Those things are solely the cherry on the cake. You are the highly valuable cake itself. The *Real Woman* knows this.

She may have grown up in a home similar to that of the *Good Girl* but somehow along the way she decided the price was too high to fit that image and so she stepped out on her own, finding a new way to live her life. With that level of independence and wisdom, she began changing her and her relationship styles. For each of us, part of being an adult is learning who you want to be in the world and how you want to present. You consciously decide whether you want to live as that more developed, aware self in a whole new world with a new way of experiencing relationships or not.

Not for a moment am I saying that this transition from *Good Girl* to *Real Woman* is necessarily easy. It often comes along with the realization that your husband was cheating, you lost out on a job to someone less qualified, you are getting a divorce, or you became seriously ill, etc. The shock, the anger, the feelings of helplessness, or feeling betrayed all call you to step back, look at the life you have created, and make a firm decision to do it differently. At times it may also be that you are just tired, really, really tired. You need a dramatic shift back into you, your life, your dreams, and your desire to live life and thrive to the fullest. Always, the shift becomes a conscious choice, not an easy one but a necessary one nonetheless.

The *Real Woman* as an embodied soul, or essence, is intrinsically holy and good. She is also kind and compassionate. She is most frequently the *Good Girl* who has become a woman, bringing the best of who she is with her. A big difference is that the *Real Woman* has learned to develop boundaries. She tends to avoid dependent and needy people knowing they are searching to be rescued not supported. She feels called to lead her life and live her purpose, not solely support others while they are avoiding theirs.

Offering a helping hand to someone in need is a good deed and it reflects the best of who she is. It is giving them a hand up. It is also a wonderfully humanitarian thing to do. Attempting to rescue someone who will not take responsibility for themselves is totally different. The *Real Woman* recognizes those folks who once you help them, create another problem, then another, then another. I am sure you know someone like that. We all do. After a while it is exhausting so why not distance early?

I routinely support causes when and where I can. I have given a room full of furniture to a family whose home burnt down. I never used that room anymore and they needed it far more than I. When I moved to a smaller home at one point, I gave a few rooms of furniture to various charities that had people waiting for the basics. I was thrilled to help. When a friend in need called because her car broke down in the winter I drove there so she could wait in a warm car for AAA to come (usually an hour or more in my experience.) Those are good deeds. I believe we all should be willing to do them in whatever form we can.

However, when another friend was consistently running late and needed me to fill in for something I only did it the first time. After the 3rd or 4th request I simply asked "What is going on that you cannot say no and you are running yourself ragged? Perpetually rescuing her would not be helping her at all. She had taken on far more than was possible because she didn't want to disappoint anyone. Where were her boundaries??? Disappoint them I say… They will survive that trauma. In fact, once she guiltily said no, they found someone else.

A friend I used to go the movies with every Friday night always showed up 10 minutes late. The first two times I waited at the popcorn stand getting progressively angrier at her. I then realized I was the crazy one not her. From that point forward, I told her I would meet her inside and save a seat. She was initially indignant yet she recovered… No more anger or resentment and not one more single ruined evening, because my anger was my issue not hers.

She was always late for everyone, everywhere. It wasn't personal and if you asked her it was never her fault. It was always someone else who made her late. You can't solve a problem someone will not even own so adapt or move on. If I had kept supporting her behavior, I would have developed resentment, anger, and a distaste for her while also losing a wonderful friendship. I have taught all my students for years that we are all a wee bit crazy. Some in their analness, some in their insecurities, some in their cleanliness, or their obsessiveness; we are all unique in our mild craziness. The trick is if you learn what yours is, you control it; it doesn't control you. You learn to compensate.

For the *Real Woman*, relationships are much more about sharing who she is with someone and walking together as they each share the adventure. Sometimes she gives 70% and sometimes the other gives 70%. The norm, however, is balanced and they are there to laugh, cry, explore, and grow into life as partners, friends, and peers. No one is carrying another.

As in all relationships there are disagreements. However, she focuses on the problem, not the person. She confronts the issue rather than creating conflict. Her understanding is that it is a problem not a crisis. This allows her to avoid any fear of abandonment or rejection. There are not good guys and bad guys in this scenario just different or conflicting ideas or wants.

Being realistic, she knows that on occasion going out with girlfriends gives her a safe place to vent, to talk about problems and find solutions she may not have considered otherwise. It also separates her from the problem far enough to see it objectively and perhaps laugh at herself.

She believes in her marriage/relationship as much as she believes in her partner. She doesn't expect perfection but loves to see how close she can get... There is an ease, comfort, and a trust. When she is annoyed, she knows she needs to look at how much of it hers and not her partners. As a hint, if he/she did the same thing yesterday and it was a non-issue and today you want to kill, it isn't about them.

What's going on with you that the reaction is so strong?

Recognizing that they can both regress to a child's mental state, when that occurs she walks away to deal with it later when the adults return. What she discovers is that the freedom from blame, shame, fear, etc. becomes what she craves in all her relationships. The more she experiences it, the more she expects it, yet understanding that the spoiled, bratty, rejected child will show up on occasion. But only for a very short visit because she recognizes when she goes to that place and deals with it as her stuff not anyone else's.

A girlfriend from NYC called a few minutes ago asking if I had a few minutes to talk. She is writing a book and wanted to talk about titles since she had too many ideas to choose from. We discussed that and then how she could use the book to get a job she wanted at a global firm through a contact she knows. We were both fed in the conversation. She then discussed the title of my book and gave me ideas on having it be provocative which is the intent and offered to hold a book launch in NYC where she would interview me and then we would do the same event when her book came out. That is an exciting friendship where we both would have won even if we had just discussed her book. It was an exhilarating conversation. These types of relationships stimulate you to become a better, more expansive, you, more enlightened and with more joy.

The challenges come when we are called to continue sharing, growing, and being there yet we may be frightened of sharing a failure, or a vulnerability all while wanting someone to love us in our humanity. It can also be frightening in loving someone who isn't perfect and who can unknowingly disappoint or hurt you on occasion simply because they are human. Courage and choice call you to remain with them whether they are a friend, lover, or spouse.

Your relationships are meant to feed you. They are intended to make you rich in the most important ways. Your relationships with yourself, your family, your friends, and even your co-workers are all meant to support you in becoming even more of who you are meant to be. They call you to keep growing. As a therapist I can tell you that you can do about 70% of your personal growth on your own. That other

30% of the growth needed requires you to be in a relationship. Any kind of healthy relationship is good. Friendship, neighbors, team-mates, lovers, etc. all fill the requirement. (Notice, however, when you hide behind your relationships with your animals in order to avoid humans.)

Relationships are like mirrors and you do not always like what you see which is why some try to go through life without any. They reflect back to you what you are putting out there. You truly get what you expect because you set it up that way. People treat you the way you trained them to treat you. If everyone in your life treats you like a servant guess why.

Not only do you train yourself how to treat you, you are showing everyone in your life how you want to be treated. Set boundaries, for them and you. When I am eating dinner, whether alone or with friends, I let everything go to voicemail. When I am visiting with friends, my phone is off. No one on this planet needs me so badly they cannot survive without me for an evening. If it is an emergency, they can call 911 and leave a message for me. No "job" needs to be attended to instantly at all times. Time off allows you to go back feeling fed and more productive.

A more in-depth question is, do you know the level of intimacy you are comfortable with? Do you ever challenge it? Do you only let people in on a surface level? Do you risk getting your heart broken by a friend or lover or do you always play it safe? Are you convinced having confidences gives people power over you or do you selectively bring in people you can trust and thus you can share anything and everything with them, so that they can actually know who you are? All of these questions are powerful when you answer honestly. The *Real Woman* isn't automatically without fear in answering them she simply pulls up her courage to do so.

Relationships, if they are to grow, call you to grow along with them. If they don't grow they will stagnate and die and eventually become a weight on your shoulders. They become an obligation rather than source of joy. When that happens you both allowed it. You both neglected it and neither of you took the initiative to say "Stop, I don't want to lose this. We need to get back to this as a priority." Skip blame. ALWAYS skip blame. Just look at options. Is it worth re-investing in? If so, go for it. If not, let go.

True, authentic, relationships are rare and a gift beyond words. If one or both of you have grown or changed your values so completely it cannot work, then bless it for the gift it was, and let it go. You can learn from every relationship you enter no matter the depth or the duration.

The woman who starts the next friendship, lover-relationship, will not be the same woman who started the last. You will have been transformed as you learned, grew, and expanded the you, you are bringing into this next one. If you were truly present, you have more skills in intimacy and a greater awareness of what you bring and/ or need in relationship and thus a whole new adventure will begin teaching you even more and making you more and more of who you are meant to be.

As a professional woman in relationships within the business world, how do you want to be seen? What kind of relationships do you want to have? I always opt for honest, authentic, with a touch of lightness, if not play. I expect others to treat me the way I treat them. I expect to be respected, valued, and appreciated. As in all my relationships, I give a bit more than expected because that is my style. They must however be clean, clear, up front and without hidden agendas, unspoken hopes perhaps, but I do not want to feel manipulated or distrustful. If I do, I leave.

No matter where you are in your growth, be gentle with yourself, because as I said before, we are never done until we go home. When you are exhausted, or vulnerable, or in fear, the *Real Woman* can fall into the *Good Girl* mindset for a wee bit. Breathe, remember the woman you have become, and call a friend if you need who truly knows you, she will quickly bring you back. It doesn't matter if you are a new entrepreneur or the President/CEO of a global organization, you are human.

When my business as a healer was getting more national attention, I was initially overwhelmed. I called a girlfriend of about 20 years at the time, and said "Barb, I feel like a fraud. I don't think I can do anything they say I can do." She said: "You're right. That time a patient's doctor cancelled surgery because you did a healing on her and she no longer needed it? That was a fluke. That time when you worked with a woman who was using a walker on the rare occasions she went out and after 6 months you had her working full time at the Boys and Girls club, a lucky break."

She went through a few other instances and by the end we were both laughing and I was back. The *Real Woman* was alive and well. We all do it. We all leave that mindset. We are human. The difference is, the more you practice the easier it is to stay away for shorter and shorter periods of time and the fewer times you leave. Welcome to humanity!

GETTING REAL:

1. Do you find all your relationships have folks who depend on you constantly?

2. Do you need to be in control of all your relationships?

3. Which girl/woman do you become when a relationship ends?

4. What are your honest expectations (not hopes) for your relationships?

5. Are you willing to become what it is you want to find?

CHAPTER NINE

LEADERSHIP

Answering the call to elevate the world.

A t this point we need to assume that the *Good Girl* is all but forgotten. That is because leadership is a position that a *Good Girl* could never successfully fill. Leadership requires hiring and firing. It requires saying no, defining boundaries, and promoting ideas others may oppose or fear. It requires arguing for your position and the need to walk into the unknown, and, it requires change. The status quo never leads. As a result, the strengths, objectivity, and personal power needed to lead would demand far too much and create unbearable stress for a *Good Girl*. This is the career and life path for the *Real Woman*.

She can lead because she is her best authentic, developed, and powerful self. She is heart and soul centered with the ability to take charge and make things happen without getting caught up in old beliefs and illusions. She is not governed by a fear of offending, hurting, or being too much for others.

As a leader you will never be "too much." When you are in fear, you may be too aggressive or too needy, but you will never be "too much."

A leader is also inner-directed. You follow your own instincts, your inner wisdom, and your own inner knowledge. Freed from other people's needs or perceptions, you can flourish under your own guidance. You study when you can and trust yourself when in fear.

When you do need advice, you ask for ideas from a trusted advisor, mentor, or an objective third party who can give you their impartial perspective on a particular problem. You know you can take the best of others' ideas, come up with a solution that works perfectly for you and then simply follow your gut. You have developed the skill to assess their opinion and then either adopt it, integrate it, or let it go.

The guidance of others is a gift you deserve since none of us is always on target with everything. When used in conjunction with your own instincts, it will expand your perspective and show you other options so that you can understand where others are coming from as well as recognize what you may not be seeing. The greater the leader is, the greater the humility, and willingness to listen, and to learn.

Leaders lead – period – out front and with authority! Leaders dare to be different; they dare to stand out to get where they want to go and where they want to take their team and their company. We cannot stand out or excel by fitting in. Fitting in keeps us in what is – leaders take us into the future, ahead of the game. Leaders and pioneers are frequently the same thing since both see potential that others don't.

Trends in business are showing ethics will play a major role in the future, people-focused businesses are far more bottom-line successful, and purpose-driven businesses are excelling. The timing is perfect. Leaders are being called to be compassionate, relationship-based, and purpose-driven team players, as well as instinctual problem solvers.

Because these leadership traits are so natural to women, it is now time for more women to enter the fields of medicine, politics, corporate business, and entrepreneurship. They can naturally make a dramatic change. In fact, they already have:

- It was the women in congress who worked across party lines, as friends, to stimulate negotiations and bring an end to the government shut-down in 2013

- We have documented improvements in organizations with women in leadership as measured by productivity, profitability, corporate culture and sustainability – in ten different categories of performance.

  McKinsey.com Women Matter. Oct. 2008

- Women-owned firms are greatly impacting the economy and generating $1.8 Trillion in economic impact while hiring 9.2 million people!

  2018 State of Women Owned Business Report

Catalyst, a leading research and advisory organization focusing on diversity writes that not only are diverse organizations more likely to retain talent, companies with higher levels of gender diversity and with HR policies and practices that focus on gender diversity are linked to lower levels of employee turnover.

> Muhammad Ali, Isabel Metz, and Carol T. Kulik, "Retaining a Diverse Workforce: The Impact of Gender-Focused Human Resource Management," Human Resource Management Journal, vol. 25, no. 4 (2015): p. 580-599.

In addition, a study of 353 of the Fortune 500 companies Catalyst says:

> Companies with a higher representation of women in senior management positions financially outperform companies with proportionally fewer women at the top. These findings support the business case for diversity, which asserts companies that recruit, retain, and advance women will have a competitive edge in the global marketplace.
> https://www.catalyst.org/media/catalyst-study-reveals-financial-performance- higher-companies-more-women-top

I can assure you, the women who have achieved this level of success are not seen as "nice" or *Good Girls* but are seen as powerful *Real Women* who are authentic, present, and inspiring. These women are not justifying their existence or their success, even if at times it feels surreal. When they are alone they may wonder how it happened or fear failure or making a mistake. They may even at times get lost and become aggressive and even cruel but recovery and "coming home" shows up sooner rather than later.

Fear and overwhelmed reflects human nature. In going forward despite those fears or flaws, they are successful because they:

- Are real women, powerful, focused, and clear on their message
- Want to create a legacy
- Are taking ownership of their ability, power, and success
- Have developed Emotional Intelligence
- Practice Mindfulness
- Develop strong teams & strong leaders around them
- Run the business – the business doesn't run them.

In describing their leadership, I have found great women leaders:

- Make it about a movement not themselves
- Develop their courage with others' support
- View challenges as opportunities to grow
- Create a culture of helpfulness and community
- Want commitment to a shared vision not to themselves
- See their leadership as an active choice for change and purpose.

They know that only by supporting each other along the way were they able to make it. Women supporting women, sharing stories, successes, fears, and difficulties, create a life-giving base of operation. I have created Think Tanks where they can complain, question, research, brainstorm together, and get support from myself and others who understand.

Supporting someone else makes things clear in your own mind. Mutual support strengthens rather than weakens everyone involved. Honest, clear, communication that is real, raw, and liberating, supporting the mindset you need to succeed in joy, with passion, power, and profitability is a necessity.

No woman can do this alone and sustain it. No woman can do this alone and still have room for herself and her relationships. *Real Women* are changing the world but we are doing it together....

GETTING REAL:

1. Are you comfortable seeing yourself as a leader?

2. If so, how would you describe yourself?

3. What is your goal as a leader?

4. What is your goal for your life?

5. Do you have a bucket list? If not, create one. Now!

CHAPTER TEN

THE GIFTS YOU BRING

Your "Why", Your "Be" and Your "Do"

For decades, we were taught to develop our CVs or our resumes by listing every pragmatic skill, training, and position we ever had. The more the merrier. A new approach to employment, especially leadership, requires that you list so much more. The so-called soft skills which at one point were considered unimportant, have taken on far greater significance. More and more organizations require these skills to qualify for any high-level leadership position.

This new leadership approach has nothing to do with your job title, but it has everything to do with who you are – how you show up - and the type of impact you have. Identifying and owning your leadership legacy is a major element of what you bring to the table; it supports you in bringing your unique qualities to the position and to all those you will be impacting. The deepest, and most enriching of the qualities you bring to any organization, especially your own, are found in your Why, your Be and your Do. The *Real Woman* lives each of them, consciously, letting them become her guiding light.

Lance Secretan, an international trainer in leadership development, has written a wonderful book, *The Spark, The Flame and The Torch* in which he discusses in detail your Why, Be & Do. The first line of self-questioning, as he sees it, becomes Why are you here? What have you come onto this earth to accomplish? If it is to be a leader, then how? What are you bringing to that role?

Take a look at your life at the moment. If you are still in remnants of the *Good Girl* stage you may feel successful, your business and your personal life may be doing fine. The next question becomes: Are you really doing what you came here to do? Are you living your purpose? Or are you still following the safe path waiting to come alive?

If it is the latter, you are still caught in the old search for safety. If so, not only are you missing out, but you are still hesitating to take risks as you go forward. Living life as it is meant to be requires taking risks on a daily basis. Those risks eliminate complacency and bring depth, joy, and a sense of accomplishment. They connect you to these three guideposts for your life.

The risks you take will be frightening (if they weren't where is the risk?) yet they are also calculated risks rather than foolish choices. As a *Real Woman* you are prepared to knowingly grow into the career and position that most suits your "Why." It is taking your desire to be a *Real Woman* to a whole new level. It is also asking you to walk a conscious spiritual journey following your soul's calling with a defined sense of purpose. I believe fully, we have come here to learn what it is we came here to teach. Every person I work with shows evidence of that.

Coming from an orphanage and then a violent home in the housing projects, I learned early that I needed to become the leader of my own life. I needed an open heart and to claim my power and self-definition as well as take risks if I was to grow beyond my environment. My initial desire even as a child, was to teach others that they were not victims and to expand their reach. I began that message in social work with children in residential treatment. I then became a psychotherapist with a thriving practice.

Simultaneously, I opened my own institute, The Institute of Healing Arts and Sciences. Teaching healers how to heal on all levels, emotionally, spiritually, and physically. Finally, I became an international speaker, coach, and consultant for leaders needing to expand their skills and rise to higher levels of success and influence. The venues have changed, and yet my "Why" never did. As with most, as I grew, how I lived it grew with me.

A question for you is, how focused or aware are you of your "Why"? In what way does it feed your passion? Your spirituality? Your joy? Blessedly, your "Why" is what lets you know you are in the right place at the right time and who doesn't love that feeling?

Once you know your why, the next question is who you want to be in living it.

You must be the leader of your personal and professional life. Taking responsibility for every choice you make rather than blaming others. In your professional life if your desire is to be a leader, or your calling is such, what kind of leader do you choose to be? Dictatorial? Supportive? Inspirational? Motivational? In planning? The Visionary? The Team Leader? The Organizational Leader? There are so many choices. Who do you, as a multidimensional being - and leader - choose to be as you bless the world?

Will you keep growing and changing? Will you grab on and hold on tight? Will you lead from fear or from compassion? Will you be at peace and through Mindfulness create a culture that supports growth, change, and personal investment from all your people, your family, or your clients?

What I have seen frequently is that the more you follow your expanding dreams, the more you expand your potential, and the more you become the best you. With every risk you take, the more strengths you discover, the more areas of growth you see, the more joy you experience, and the more alive you become.

With your Why and your Be in place, the final part of this process is looking at how you want to live them. It is what you Do to bring that why and that woman you choose to be to the world. You are here with permission to be the woman you chose to become in the process. I showed you above how I have lived my Why. Now it's your turn.

Take a moment and look over your life. Have you been living your "Why" while being and becoming the person you want to be? If not, gently look to see how you have betrayed yourself. How did you limit yourself? How did you get lost in your own life? How frequently did you settle for surviving rather than living?

I have met many women who got caught in a safe job that supported them and they gradually acquiesced to a point where they lost touch with their reason for living, their purpose, passion, and joy. In losing themselves they lost touch with who they wanted to be as well.

Many physicians entered medicine to heal, and/or bring pain relief to others. After paying off student loans, with massive malpractice insurance premiums as well, they feel as if their life is one of patient reports and new computer systems. They are in the field they felt called to, they followed their why and yet who they have become as an administrator rather than a healer feels as if what they are doing is not at all what they envisioned.

In working with them I ask, "If this isn't feeding your soul, if you are in the field you still choose but are not doing your calling, can you begin by backing up to discover the person you have become vs. the person you wanted to be? One client of mine thought she was very much a detail person. In working together, she discovered that she is very much a visionary, a thought leader, who wants to change how medicine is offered to those in low income areas.

When she talks about it she becomes alive. Her passion is vibrant and a joy to watch. It is clear she now needs to do what she is called to do at this point in her life. She and her work have been transformed. As she grew, even without seeing it, how she lived her why, what she is now called to do, evolved as had mine. Has yours? Sometimes we can get lost while doing or living our purpose, we can get lost in the mundane and lose us and the dream.

Other times we need to take a detour temporarily. If at times you took a position simply because you needed money coming in, fine. Knowing that you did that as a means of paying the bills, supporting a family, etc. doesn't mean you lost your dream unless you allowed it to go. It could also have been the opportunity to stop, breathe, and catch up with the specifics of how you wanted to get to your goal. Detours can be a great gift. They are only a means of self-betrayal when you let go of yourself along with disconnecting from your "Why" "Be" and "Do."

Take time through Mindfulness to see if you as a *Real Woman* are living yours. If you have gotten lost in bringing who you are to the world, know the world desperately needs you. We are in a time when *Real Woman* are being called to be everything they are capable of so that we can have the greatest impact imaginable on a world that is spinning and at a loss for values that mean something.

Our skills in collaboration, our ability to lead with compassion and to call others to their leadership as well, are gifts the world needs NOW - however and wherever you share them.

GETTING REAL:

1. Do you now have an awareness of your purpose, your driving force?

2. What type of person do you want to become as you live your life?

3. Generous? Passionate? Inquisitive? Something else?

4. What are you doing to support that happening while also making the world a better place?

5. Do you see this as a spiritual journey of purpose or random births?

6. What it is that motivates you?

CHAPTER ELEVEN

THE NEW LEADERSHIP

A Style all Your Own

I n becoming the *Real Woman* your life changes in ways, you never anticipated. I found, like many before me, that at this point we rarely get the opportunity to be the follower, or submissive. In spite of ourselves we end up in leadership positions in clubs, jobs, even places of worship. That is the result of both our natural tendencies at this point, as well as because of how we are seen energetically.

Embrace who you are, or who you have become, and proudly come along with the all those others who have chosen to be that *Real Woman.* We have differentiated ourselves and as we continue to grow we will be doing so more and more.

Because of my varied professional background, I have experienced a wide variety of approaches to leadership. The old concept of power-over or top-down has been shown to have many built-in flaws which makes it imperative to look at other options. Thankfully, just as there are many approaches and styles of personalities, there are also many approaches and styles of leadership.

As you read those I am presenting notice which one or two are your top styles. Which traits of each are your strengths? Within those, which traits need further development? Your top one or two primary styles will be your natural fallback at times of high stress. With developed Emotional Intelligence and experience, you recognize when you go into defense and you know how to get out of it quickly before any negative ramifications or regrets.

In business whether in your own company, or in another, you may be asked to lead in a position that doesn't at all fit who you are. If you work in corporate, never take the position that doesn't fit simply as a great "avenue up" if it isn't your strength. We have all known people in the wrong jobs and the price is high, as is the failure rate. Consequently, identifying and valuing your approach and strengths in leadership can save you a lot of heartache, money, and stress.

Becoming a *Real Woman* requires honesty with yourself as well as with others. Some strengths you can develop and you should. For the other strengths that may be lacking, if you are an entrepreneur, you hire in or look elsewhere for that support. Own your strengths and hire people to compensate for your limitations in particular areas.

As an example, not everyone has the skills or mind function to be the organizational leader, developing systems and subsets of systems, for every program that gets presented. This is not a defect, simply a style of leadership that isn't yours. You have others. Know which ones you possess. There are many people who love having any one of these styles of leadership. Thank God they exist and that you can hire them as a team member or a consultant.

An important point to remember is that each of these styles is an aspect of your personality, not your essence. They do not define your character or your intrinsic value they simply show you and others where your strengths are in terms of personal and professional leadership. However, I highly recommend that you balance your personality and leadership style as much as possible by strengthening your competence in each, even minimally, so that you can call on any one of them if needed in a pinch.

A side note I would like to mention here, frequently I have clients tell me they are one way at home and yet totally different at work, and vice versa. Let me tell you now that is a lie you are telling yourself. Your style is your style. You may have far more tolerance in one location or another yet when leadership is needed there is only one-two styles you will call on.

Here is a brief overview:

THOUGHT LEADER

She is the gift that can think far out of the box in problem solving as well as in bringing your product or interest beyond your wildest dreams.

TEAM LEADER

She teaches and incorporates the corporate culture while creating leaders throughout a high functioning team.

SUPPORTIVE LEADER

She never wants to be seen as the face or official leader of a company yet she is the one who will guarantee at all personal costs that every project is completed, everything is working, and the Visionary leader shines.

VISIONARY LEADER

She is absolutely charismatic and loves being the recognized face of an organization. She is the Dream Holder and Visionary who does what needs to get done to take her organization as far as it can go and further.

ORGANIZATIONAL LEADER

She naturally creates systems and processes for the company or any group she is in. She is creating to-do lists and structures while others are just beginning a discussion.

Try this Self-Assessment Leadership Tool that I have created to support your understanding of your leadership style. Know that no matter how many years you may have been in leadership, when you are vulnerable, in fear or exhaustion, you can stumble.

If you are new in claiming the *Real Woman* that you have always been, this is an introduction to a world that can support your growth, success, and living your purpose. Whether strengthening the vulnerabilities in your particular style or developing other types, know that balance is what allows you to live a peaceful, joyful, and ever-developing journey.

There is no right or wrong type, only different styles of leadership. If you can, with a pencil, check each little point that applies to you. When you have finished, notice the styles with the most checks. Standardly, there are two primary styles that stand out.

They define what makes your leadership style yours. The others are available if needed but only in a pinch unless you choose to develop them further. Always, however, your top two will be your default, your strengths, and your greatest vulnerabilities in leadership.

If you prefer, you can download this **Leadership Self-Assessment Tool,** for free, at: **http://www.askdrdorothy.com/**

THE 5 ARCHETYPES OF LEADERSHIP

STRENGTH	VULNERABILITIES	BASIC BELIEFS	RELATIONSHIP PATTERNS
THOUGHT LEADER			
o Insightful sees Big Picture o Creative – Brilliant o Thinks Out of the Box o Idealistic	o Constant Fear/ Anxiety o Sees Life as Unsafe o Disorganized o Unfocused/ Scattered o Can Be Hypervigilant	o Life Is Limitless o Anything Is Possible o Life Is Dangerous o I Am Trapped and Disconnected o I Don't Fit In	o Highly Perceptive o Can Be Great Conversationalist o Can Isolate into Ideas - Aloof o Limited Ability for True Intimacy/ Connection o Can Be suspicious
TEAM			
o Community/Culture Builder o Great Motivator o Develops Individual leaders o Develops a Solid Team o Understands People's Needs and Wants	o Not Recognizing Own Needs o Fears Abandonment o Holds on Too Long o Can be Seen as Greedy o Expects Others to Fill Their Needs	o We are All in This Together. o There's No One Here for Me. o Everyone's Going to Leave Me. o I'm All Alone o I Can't Get Enough.	o Safe to be Around o People Easily Confide in Them. o Clings to Others. o Consumed with Their Own Needs. o Others initially take care of them then abandonment.
SUPPORTIVE			
o Loyal o Persevering o Hard Worker o Capable of Great Love/Caring o Playful	o Passive Aggressive o Goes to Martyrdom o Illusion of Victimization/ Powerless o Sees Themselves as limited o Tends to Experience Being Overwhelmed	o People are Good o I'm not Really Important o I must obey/go along with others to be valued o I would if I could but I can't o I am powerless	o Unconditionally loving/caring o Always ready and willing to help o Great ability to forgive o Co-Dependency o Gives excessively then blames others for taking

STRENGTH	VULNERABILITIES	BASIC BELIEFS	RELATIONSHIP PATTERNS
VISIONARY			
o Powerful recognized leader o Charismatic o Powerful speaker o Generous o Cool under fire.	o Fears any loss of control o Fears not being good enough o Fears not being powerful enough o Fear of being controlled o Feels betrayed easily	o I can achieve anything I set out to do o I must never show hurt/vulnerability to anyone o You are with me or against me o If I don't have control others will o It is my way or the wrong way	o Lovingly protective and supportive o You can only be close to me if you look up to me o Doesn't let others get too close o Wants all the power while others have all the responsibility o Insists upon being supported.
ORGANIZATIONAL			
o High Achiever o Very Organized o Self-Confident o Very Responsible o Passionate- Adventurous	o Perfectionist o Easily Angered o Great Difficulty Expressing Emotions o Hides in Work o Excessively Competitive	o Life is Meant to be Organized and Highly Functional o I Must Be Perfect in Order to be Loved o Love is Conditional o Chaos/Drama means Death/ Danger o It is More Important to Appropriate and Perfect Than Real	o Capable of Deep Connection o Others Feel Energized Around Them o Trouble Believing They are Loved – Unconditionally o Longs for Tenderness Yet Can Be Uncomfortable with Affection o Afraid of Being Hurt – Not Being Good Enough

This Tool is the basis of several programs. It could take an hour or even a two day workshop (I offer both.) to fully understand the implications of your results. However, I do want you to at least see what is possible and how skilled you are in these styles. In addition, I want you to recognize your limitations as not simply personal weaknesses but as traits that are intrinsic to your leadership style. This provides hope and possibilities for growth and you never have too much of either.

GETTING REAL:

1. What are your strongest styles?

2. Are they what your job calls for?

3. Is there anyone that you judged? (I would guess it needs work if you did.)

4. What are your strongest traits?

5. What are your weakest?

CHAPTER TWELVE

GOING FORWARD

Time to change the world!

As a *Real Woman* you are free to go forward and create whatever opportunities you desire. You have let go of trying to please everyone and looking around to see what is acceptable. Having incorporated the warmth and generosity of the *Good Girl* while simultaneously releasing her ability to negatively impact your life, you are free to go wherever and whenever your inner knowing calls you.

The artificial constraints and weights that were holding you down have been released. When you are in the *Real Woman* mindset they no longer have a hold on you. If you do slip back, you have tools to get out fast. Make sure you use them.

In the mindset of the *Real Woman* you listen to you own voice, you speak so that everyone you meet knows you have claimed that status. Using your voice to share who you are, without apologizing, justifying, or explaining shows your comfort in your own skin.

With a daily practice of Mindfulness and a commitment to continuously growing in your Emotional Intelligence, your inner strengths are consciously present. Living in the present is a gift you give yourself as well. Acknowledging your shadow side rather than running from it or denying it truly empowers you. Take your rage if you have it and use it as fuel to fly forward in a clear concise way. Use your insecurities as a call to go inside or to call a friend, whatever you need.

In all of your relationships, know you are as important, knowledgeable, and powerful as your partner. Choose only those who can appreciate you in your fullness never anyone who wants to "help" you learn how to do you "right." Relationships are there to feed you, to call you to your best self while also being that safe place where you can cry, rant, play, collapse, and be all powerful. In essence, to be yourself, in every amazing, passionate way you know how.

Your leadership is yours. Whether in your personal life or your professional life, working in collaboration or working alone, you need to know where you want to go and who you want to become so you can get all the guidance you need from within and without....

Let your Purpose be your strongest guide. Always stay in alignment with it. What you do and who you become is the byproduct of your commitment to that Purpose. What supports you in living it? What supports you as it transitions you to its next expression? For me that transition was going from being a psychotherapist to an Executive Coach, Consultant, and Trainer. What's yours?

There is no set picture of what you should do with your life other than following your Purpose. Being free to move into whatever the next step may be is liberating beyond words. As the CEO of my own company, I believe in creating one year and five-year plans. They give me a focus, a filter through which I can assess which opportunities would be best for me and my company.

I also know, however, from decades in this work, that at any point as I am moving toward my defined goals, an opportunity I never could have imagined may present itself. If I use the tools of mindfulness, reflection, and prayer, and a whole new avenue appears and which Spirit, my heart and my soul are calling me towards, I'm in! I love the adventure, the experiences and the growth that will come from it. I am always fully aware that the strengths developed while following my business plan are what made me ready for this next unanticipated adventure.

A practice of spiritual detachment, releasing a hold on all things, allows you to step back and realize that you are not this life you have created. You are not your family, friends, career, or home. You are so much more. You are far greater than all this. If you believe in reincarnation, this one lifetime is only one experience in your soul's many adventures. Looking at it from that perspective, whatever it is that calls you to grow and become more and more of who you are meant to be, is where you need to be.

Trust your inner knowing. Trust the life you have created. You have a responsibility to it, but it does not define you. It is simply an environment, a context, you have created in which to live your Why as you become the you, you are called to Be, and doing whatever it is you are here to Do.

It is so easy to forget that you exist on many levels as an energetic, spiritual, emotional, intellectual, and physical being. Nonetheless, every element of who you are needs to be fed. You have a responsibility for the self-care of each and every part. It can be overwhelming at times, but it is also so very invigorating. As a communal being you also have a responsibility to consciously walk this earth with all those who co-exist here with you.

An important part of that communal responsibility is in mentoring those who are following you. Ask yourself, who, male or female, can you mentor? Who can you, to the extent that you are able, support along the way? How can you make the road easier, less frightening, and less lonely for someone else? Those you mentor come and go. It may be for one conversation, one project. The time is irrelevant. The ownership of your skills in mentoring, of being that person, that other-focused person who gives from her fulness not depletion, who gives because she has so much to offer just in being her, makes you so much more. It calls you to own that *Real Woman* you have become. It reinforces for you how much you have grown, learned, and risked. Mentoring others is an affirmation for you that you did it! You made it!

In a world that has reached a peak of hatred, bias, cruelty, and lack of true spiritual connection, you are a much-needed force. Know your limits, be aware of the demands on you and chose with great discernment. With whatever resources are left, know what it is that you can share to support this world becoming a better place.

As I said earlier, 70% of our growth comes from developing a healthy relationship with yourself and your place in the world. The other 30% comes from being in relationship. Your relationship with the world is immeasurably important. Take time to retreat when needed. Take a day for pajamas, movies, popcorn and wine. Take that day or evening we talked about earlier with your closest friends when you can spend an evening, or part of one, whining and complaining, or doing drama and rage. Get it out of your system in a safe, fun way. Most importantly, take time for retreats to separate from your life and to rediscover the depths of your soul but after, remember that you are a citizen of the world. It needs you.

A case in point, although this ages me, I was a child before Title IX. When I was growing up boys always had sports. Girls never had the sports funding because it wasn't considered important or needed. Title IX changed that. I excelled at math and yet was told that it was a boy's subject, so I should focus on English or history instead. Thankfully that point has changed somewhat and yet we are still putting in a concerted effort to support the inclusion of women in STEM. We have come far and yet...

We are in a culture that supports bias and the guidelines to support equal pay have been eliminated. The vast majority of our senators are male and there is a call for women to be grateful rather than participatory, to be led rather than to lead. At a hearing recently, a senator asked a potential Supreme Court judge to tell her of any laws he knew of which governed a man's body. He could think of none. She implied clearly that there are too many that exist governing a woman's body. We are not there yet...

The insidiousness of these biases enters our personal and professional relationships. We are called to be a *Good Girl* and let the changes come when they do. Another choice is to stand up in strength as a *Real Woman* and get those changes made. Whichever choice you make will have an effect on every relationship you are in because it will transform you or cause you to stagnate. If we are going to help transform this world, stagnation is not an option only action is. Choose action.

The planet needs it; our sisters throughout the world need it. No one on this planet should be without needed health care. No one on this planet should be without drinking water; food; freedom; the opportunity to work; and a habitable home. *Real Women* have the ability to join with *Real Men* and change all the inequities that exist. Our planet has the skills, what it lacks however is commitment from those who could readily solve these problems. The insecure need for power-over, egos, hatred, fear, greed, and bias are the blocks to moving forward. It seems women are being called in yet again to unblock progress from being made. Being ready, becoming the *Real Woman* is our next step.

Our willingness to make people uncomfortable when we confront them with truth is our strength.

Our ability to rely on others to collaborate with us is our tool. Our willingness to look in the mirror and own what we see becomes our greatest protector. No one can hold something over you if you already own it. We know we are flawed while also knowing we are ever-growing. Our spiritual, humanitarian, approach to loving and change makes us powerful beyond words. Calling people to compassion, warmth, and servant leadership, is calling them to their best self. That needs to be our way.

I don't believe in fighting those who oppose me. I believe in letting them battle the air while I walk around them and keep going. Don't waste energy on someone who doesn't want a problem solved, they only want to fight. The win is their joy making the issue irrelevant. Leave them in the fight. You aren't even needed there. They fight simply to win. Bringing your best self calls the others to live up to your expectations because in truth their best self will be in the same place.

My prayer for all of us as we go forward in whatever way we can is that we work in unison to eliminate the call for any girl or woman to betray herself by being the *Good Girl.* Our calling as embodied souls, as pure essence, is to own our power, our voice, and our inner-knowing, along with our passion in making this world a place of *Real Women* and *Real Men* who together can bring to life a journey of faith, humor, and justice for all who walk this world.

We are called to love, to live our lives, and to passionately develop this life we are creating. We do it all, one risk, one dream, and one leadership decision at a time. Remember being a leader is not what you do; it is who you are.

If we are to change this world, owning our leadership, our voice, and its impact is the way to do it. What that looks like in context, style, and presentation is solely up to you. It will be informed by your Purpose. Whatever the path, it requires claiming your voice with certainty, your intuitive life-transforming gifts, your life experiences, and your knowledge as you live your dreams for your future and that of the world. Go in peace, power, and passion. You deserve no less.

The *Real Women* will change the world and we will do it together, as one, while being the developed, powerful, authentic, women we are!

ABOUT THE AUTHOR

As the founder of 4 companies, Dr. Dorothy has first-hand knowledge of the challenges facing women in business. In addition, as an Executive Leadership Coach/Consultant, she has supported women from all levels of success, Park Ave, NYC to a small town in Maine. Consequently, patterns are readily understood as she brings extensive wisdom, knowledge, and experience to the table.

Dorothy A. Martin-Neville, PhD, speaker, author, consultant/master coach, and frequent radio, podcast, and television guest in numerous countries, is past-president of the National Speakers Association - CT and on the Board of Directors of various organizations, expanding her understanding of women in positions of leadership. A psychotherapist, Dorothy was in practice for 25+ years.

Combining, her recognition that mindset and communication skills set us apart with her ability to make the complicated simple, Dorothy is someone to learn from so you can live a life of purpose, power, and passion in the realization that anything is possible if you are willing to look in the mirror, grow, risk, and make any changes necessary. As you will see, your mindset and ability to communicate make you invisible or make your presence known - it's your choice - just make sure it's a presence you want to claim.

For Dorothy, it was a presence claimed from growing up in an orphanage, living in an alcoholic home in the housing projects of South Boston, being a Catholic nun, an international airline stewardess, a wife, mother, pioneer in integrative health care in the United States, a medical school instructor, graduate professor and so much more.

In providing training programs, workshops, keynotes, or Executive Coaching, Dr. Dorothy brings the best of herself, in her full authentic Real Woman style with humor, faith, and wisdom.

Start today – in going forward as the Real Woman you are called to be. Dorothy can be reached at dorothy@askdrdorothy.com or through her website:: askdrdorothy.com

Made in the
USA
Columbia, SC